No one wants a confrontation with the IRS. With their sophisticated computers, special codes, and secret sources of information, you don't stand a chance. Or do you?

Now a former IRS criminal investigator reveals how the system really works . . . who gets audited and why . . . how agents think and what they look for . . . how to avoid trouble and handle an audit . . . the truth about informers . . . civil versus criminal cases . . . and how IRS evidence can fall apart.

Before you step into the ring, you need to know the rules, train with an expert, and understand your opponent. This insider's guide will show you how to come out fighting—and win!

IN THIS CORNER—
THE
IRS

J. R. Price
with
Valerie Putney

A DELL BOOK

Published by
Dell Publishing Co., Inc.
1 Dag Hammarskjold Plaza
New York, New York 10017

Dell ® TM 681510, Dell Publishing Co., Inc.

ISBN: 0-440-13970-8

Printed in the United States of America

First printing—January 1981

This Book Is Dedicated to
the American Taxpayer . . .

. . . and if you're a
*non*taxpayer—good luck!

TABLE OF CONTENTS

"The IRS Wants YOU"

It's a fight you never wanted; you don't even know the rules. Yet here you are in the same ring with this oversized opponent who's about to bleed you dry. . . .

"In this corner, the I . . . R . . . S . . . !" The reverberating announcement sounds like a death sentence.

The giant fist is about to strike. Your first impulse is to close your eyes tight and hope unconsciousness comes soon. But instead you do just the opposite. Awakening with a start, you realize it was just a dream, brought on by one irritating letter from the Internal Revenue Service.

What can they want of you now? As if paying your taxes weren't enough, the IRS is implying that you may have done so improperly. It's bad enough that they take such a large portion of your income right out from under you; must they also accuse you of cheating? What gall! What arrogance! What *power*!

No matter how diligently you try to comply with the law, it seems the IRS can always find something to accuse you of. And what they do to you when they find one undocumented deduction, one undeducted document—fines, prison bars, seizure of property

. . . they can ruin your life. You read about it all the time in the papers, hear it from those sober-looking newscasters reporting the terrible fate of the latest victim of IRS. No wonder you're having nightmares!

As a responsible taxpayer, you would never think of turning down an invitation from the IRS, especially when it's worded so politely: "You are hereby required to appear . . ." before a man who can turn your tax return inside out, quote tax laws you've never even heard of, and wring even more money out of you than you thought you owed in the first place. Faced by so imposing a personage, what's a poor, uninformed taxpayer to do?

Most taxpayers just accept the IRS's findings without question—mainly because they don't know what to ask, or where the examiner could have gone wrong. Correcting this unbalanced situation was one of the primary reasons for writing this book. But unlike other books of advice to taxpayers, this one does not attempt to help you to build tax shelters or develop extra deductions nor to defraud the government or attack its system of taxation. It is rather a compilation of practical, useful information about the fundamental workings of the Internal Revenue Service, gleaned from over six years as a special agent in the Criminal Investigation Division (formerly, Intelligence Division).

According to J. R. Price, on whose experience this book is based, many taxpayers could have saved money if they had taken the time to ask the right questions, or provide pertinent information—either to IRS or to an accountant or attorney. But before you can ask questions, you need to have a few answers: "How long should I keep records? What's the difference between civil and criminal violations? Can they make me pay taxes I don't really owe? Under what circumstances can they penalize me? How do I find out what they have on me?" These and many other questions are asked by taxpayers all the time. This book was intended to provide some clear, straightforward answers.

This is by no means a comprehensive guide; it would take at least ninety-nine and a half large volumes to cover all possible instances of taxpayer-IRS interaction. Rather, it is designed to give the average taxpayer who files individual U. S. Tax Return 1040 the basic information he needs to deal effectively with the divisions he's most likely to encounter. We do not presume to replace a competent accountant or tax attorney, either of whom can provide individualized advice beyond the scope of a general-information book. Having digested the contents herein, you will not become an expert, but you should have a sound working knowledge of the IRS's functions and intentions, should they ever confront you.

"Working on this book has been a great learning experience," says coauthor Valerie Putney, a freelance writer whose only prior contact with the IRS has been as a taxpayer filing a joint return with her husband. It is her lack of expertise in tax matters that distinguishes the style of this book from that of typical government publications. The theory was: If she can understand it, so can you.

A note on gender: Whenever you encounter "he" "him" or "man," you may assume that these words could be applied to a person of either sex, except where specifically noted.

In order to aid comprehension, numerous examples and anecdotes have been included in the text. While most examples have a basis in fact, names and events have been fictionalized (except stated court decisions), to protect the privacy of those whose cases were selected. In each illustration, however, the consequences are based on existing laws, rules, and regulations contained in the Internal Revenue Code. We have attempted to concentrate on those laws and procedures which are likely to remain in effect; however, there is no guarantee that some of them will not change at some future date.

If you want to learn how to fill out a tax return or how to reduce your tax liability, this book will be of little use—although it does contain a few clues. However, if you would rather have the Internal Revenue Service stay in its own corner, where you can understand it—step right in, and let a former special agent be your trainer.

GREENSBORO, NORTH CAROLINA
DECEMBER 1979

PART I

How to Deal
with a Monster

"Bureaucracy." The very word conjures up terrifying images of a monstrous maze of hopelessly tangled red tape. Yet, however much we may malign this complex and pervasive system of ours, however imperceptibly the wheels of progress seem to turn, somehow America still works. We have willingly allowed ourselves to be led by what has come to be known as "Big Government," a system which, thanks to its built-in mechanisms for self-perpetuation, is practically incapable of being overthrown.

A lot of bureaucrats feel terribly secure behind their seemingly impregnable walls of red tape. But what about We, the People on the outside looking in? We, the People who pay the bureaucrats' salaries, are not being treated with the kind of respect normally afforded those who foot the bill. In fact, the average American quakes in fear at the thought of facing our Goliath of a government when it turns its attention upon him. After all, "They" have the power, the glory, the national budget, the military services, and an army of PR men on their side. How can you hope to overcome such formidable odds?

By knowing in advance what you're dealing with,

that's how. The powers that be may look indestructible from the outside, but there are ways to get through to them. After all, the bureaucracy and all its intricately connected sub-bureaucracies were created by mortals, and so are capable of being understood by mortals. The trick is simply to discard the masses of nonessentials that tend to obscure, and then extract those jewellike nuggets of law that can truly enlighten: the essential facts. Such mining is even possible to accomplish with one of our biggest monsters, the Internal Revenue Service.

While other bureaucrats are almost completely isolated from the public they are supposedly serving, IRS agents interact constantly with We, the People—at least, the lower echelons do. Since they go about their tax-collecting and -examining chores on a daily basis, they have naturally become much more adept at tax matters than mere taxpayers who only come into contact with them occasionally. No wonder the IRS always seems to have the upper hand! But, even though this bureau is part of an even larger bureaucracy—the Treasury Department, whose secretary in turn reports to the president—you can still talk back to them, if you know how. After all, it's not as if you're trying to communicate with the whole United States government; just one bureau of it—and one (or possibly two) even smaller divisions of that. There. You've already eliminated a lot of nonessentials.

To be sure, you can't deal with the IRS as you would with an individual or even a large corporation. But, as in personal interaction, your ability to predict your adversary's behavior has a lot to do with how well your confrontations turn out . . . and in whose favor. One guiding principle is: When you must deal with an entity larger than you, their procedures will predominate. Since they won't play your game, you should learn theirs. Knowing how they operate can give you a definite edge, allowing you to meet them not as a victim, but as an equal.

You may not like the idea of your government spending ever-larger shares of your hard-earned money on an infinite array of wasteful and unnecessary programs. And you may like even less the agency that makes it possible. This book does not defend the IRS, it just offers a realistic means of getting along with a monster that seems destined to be part of our lives. If you have to live with it anyway, you may as well have some ammunition.

Once you've filed your tax returns and paid your taxes, the IRS may never want anything more to do with you. On the other hand, they might latch onto you and refuse to let go until they've dragged you through a court case. In between lie various other punitive measures, ranging from incomprehensible communications not even bureaucrats can understand to the dread tax collector who sells your business, car, and home before he's through with you. You are probably vaguely aware of these options; perhaps you are wondering under what circumstances they could be applied to you. Beyond your curiosity wait anxiety and fear. It all bubbles to the surface the day you mail in your 1040.

CHAPTER 1

The 1040 Blues

It was a proud day for Benny Fischel. Not only had he just performed his patriotic duty, but it had cost him no more than the price of a postage stamp. And it was still a full two weeks before deadline! Benny had never mailed in his tax return so early in his life.

He listened contentedly as the big blue mailbox swallowed his neatly filled-in 1040, confident that it contained nothing the least bit suspicious. The IRS would be so impressed with Benny Fischel's brilliant return, they could not possibly find fault with it.

Or could they?

Now that the tax return lay irretrievably imprisoned in that mailbox, Benny began to have second thoughts. It had seemed so innocent last night when he signed it, but now that it was on its way to the government, the old doubts crept into Benny's conscience once again.

"It was OK to list Grandma as an exemption, wasn't it?" he asked himself. "After all, she does live with us; Ernie Potshot always claims *his* mother, and he's never had any trouble, even though she spends two months in Florida every winter. So my brother pays her doctor bills, and half her food bills. If he wants her as a tax deduction, let *him* put up with the old lady day in and day out. . . ." It sounded perfectly logical to Benny; he was sure any tax auditor would agree. But then he had to remind himself that his return would never get that far.

He couldn't help but cast one last backward glance at the big blue box that marked the beginning of his tax return's journey. So preoccupied was Benny with figures, he barely noticed the black-and-gray Chevy heading straight for him as he crossed the street. Screeching brakes and honking horns startled him temporarily back into the present. But no sooner had he reached the curb than another thought occurred to him:

"Did I claim the right amount of medical expenses for Minnie's surgery? What if I can't prove them? She paid for a lot of her medicine in cash. Well, it was still a medical expense, I certainly have a right to that deduction. But what if the IRS disallows it? They can't really make me pay taxes I don't owe, can they? . . . Ooops, there I go again, worrying about being audited. No way they'll come after me, when so many other people are intentionally falsifying their returns. Those are the ones the IRS should be chasing. Anyhow, they can't audit all ninety million of us taxpayers, can they? What are the chances they'd pick me? One in a hundred thousand, maybe? So what am I worried about?"

Reassured once more, Benny hurried on to his office, almost colliding with a mob of bargain hunters swarming into the sale at Polly's Paraphernalia. "Everybody wants to save money these days," Benny thought as he watched the eager crowd descend on

Polly's bargains. "It's the same way with taxes," he reasoned. "Pay your fair share, but don't overdo it. No sense giving the government more than you owe." But somehow Benny still couldn't quite shake the guilt he felt about claiming all those deductions.

"Maybe that makes them suspicious. But they were mine to claim, they can't take them away from me. Otherwise why would they have all those laws that say we can take them? So maybe I don't have written proof that I paid Cousin Lawrence five hundred dollars for checking out that supplier for me. I still paid him, even if it was in cash. Of course, he's not going to list it as income on *his* return. I can't believe Lawrence still hasn't opened a checking account. I suppose the IRS wouldn't believe it, either. Oh, God, maybe I shouldn't have claimed that expense. . . ."

A wave of panic struck Benny Fischel. For one wild moment he wanted to run back to the seat of his concern and snatch away that envelope containing what amounted to a confession to the U.S. Government. "Why didn't I just take the standard deduction?" Benny thought. "Well, I can always think of somebody else to blame," he decided, now practically convinced he would be audited . . . or worse.

Entering his office dejected instead of exhilarated, he glanced wearily at the stacks of last year's financial records he still had not refiled since filling out the tax forms the night before. His first impulse was to sweep them all into the trash and never have to think about taxes again. "Now, there's an idea. Let them think I'm dead, and I'll never pay taxes again." But once again sanity intervened, as Benny began putting his records away. "How long did that accountant say I should keep them?" he wondered.

The sight of those canceled checks, receipts, bills, ledgers, and miscellaneous financial data brought back still more memories. He thought of the deductions he had claimed but couldn't prove, the others he had wanted to take but didn't dare, the tax advice he'd given his daughter that he wasn't at all sure about anymore, and the business expenses he may have overestimated—just slightly. "Individually, they're all pretty minor, but add them together and I look like some kind of criminal. Omigod! What if my bookie snitches? What happens if they catch me? Will they smother me with fines and penalties? Maybe it's better to pay a little extra now than wait till they jack up my bill later on. I wonder how much more they would charge? What if I can't pay it all? Will they investigate me? How will I know what they have on me?"

At last, the biggest fear of all, the one Benny had been trying hardest to ignore, surfaced: "Will they throw me in jail? What then?" Stripes, rows and rows of parallel lines, flooded into Benny's tortured mind—horrifying images of prison bars and jailbird's garb, and a dead end to a promising career.

Outside in the street a mail truck passed by, carrying the tax return that had seemed so airtight when Benny signed it last night. Where was that feeling now, that wonderful sensation of a job well done? The further that mail truck traveled, the closer Benny felt to his own doom. As the truck sped out of sight, Benny's searching eyes fell upon the calendar: "April 1," it read. That was the postmark which would appear on his tax return. It was supposed to be his little joke on the IRS. But now he had the feeling that it was he who was the April fool.

Benny Fischel's predicament should strike a familiar chord in the hearts of millions of American taxpayers. You, too, may have experienced similar doubts, misconceptions, or fears upon mailing in your tax return. Even if you've sought expert advice from people who are supposed to know taxes, you might still feel a wave of apprehension creep into your nerve endings as you send in that return. You may have the best accountant in town, but that doesn't mean he knows all the answers. After all, even accountants get audited sometimes.

Most Americans would prefer never to have to deal directly with the tax-collecting arm of the federal government, and will go out of their way to stay out of its way. When taxpayers do initiate contact, it is most often to learn how to do something they do not particularly want to do—fill out tax returns. The IRS is glad to comply with these requests, but they will not necessarily accept responsibility for the accuracy of the information they supply. Following the advice of tax experts—even when supplied by the agency that should know best—does not guarantee freedom from adjustment by the IRS.

No matter whose advice you follow, you're the one who will be held responsible for paying your own taxes. Maybe you consulted the IRS's own annual Publication 17, "Your Federal Income Tax," an understandable (at least by IRS standards), up-to-date reference to tax-return rules and regulations available at little or no charge at most IRS offices. 3.1 million copies of these handy manuals were distributed in 1979, along with a million and a half copies of Publication 334, "Tax Guide for Small Business." Or perhaps you phoned the IRS either locally or at their toll-free information number, where the error rate is about three percent, according to the IRS Commissioner's Report of 1979. A trained accountant or tax lawyer should know the score when it comes to taxes, but sometimes even they can lead you astray. And if you just accepted the word of your salesman neighbor or brother-in-law—good luck!

Even among Internal Revenue Servants themselves there can be some degree of disagreement. To drive home the point, journalists have taken fictitious data to several IRS offices in search of advice, only to turn up a variety of different responses. "How much tax should I pay on X income with Y deductions?" the reporter asks. Answers have ranged from zero to hundreds of dollars. Now, if even IRS can't come up with a definitive answer, what's a poor, uninformed taxpayer to do?

Like Benny Fischel, your imagination may begin to conjure up any number of terrifying scenarios that might not even be justified. Even if the IRS does decide to examine your return, they may find little or nothing to adjust. So those frightening confrontations you envisioned could turn out to be little more than a slight inconvenience. Still, when the Internal Revenue Service initiates contact, it can be a major source of trepidation if you don't understand how the agency functions. Even if you do, the thought of facing the IRS can send a chill down your spine. Just knowing the different IRS divisions, and what each one does, can be of some comfort in such trying times. The three divisions that commonly initiate contact with the public are: 1) the Collection Division's revenue officers; 2) the Examination Division, consisting of tax auditors and revenue agents; and 3) the Criminal Investigation Division, consisting of special agents. This book deals primarily with the latter two, plus a few helpful facts about the Appellate Division.

As for revenue officers (also known as tax collectors), there are so many different individual situations that can crop up when they come to collect taxes or secure returns, a book like this one could not possibly cover them all. Revenue officers do have the authority to seize property and garnishee wages to satisfy overdue tax bills; but if you have no way to pay, compromises or time-payment plans can sometimes be arranged by an appointee of your district director. The amount of time a revenue officer allows you for meeting your liability depends largely on how much effort he thinks you are making. If you're honestly (in his judgment) trying to pay your debt, he's likely to go easier on you. Beyond that your best course (besides paying up) may be to seek the assistance of a good tax lawyer. Remember, the revenue officer's job is to collect outstanding taxes and check on delinquent returns, not to question their justification, so it does little good to argue with him about your tax liability. You might pick up a copy of the free government publication "The Collection Process," available at most IRS offices, if you want more information about how taxes are collected.

You may have heard all sorts of horror stories

about the big bad tax collector depriving people of their livelihoods, but taxpayers' troubles usually originate not with revenue officers, but with the agents who actually compute tax liabilities. These agents work out of the divisions that examine, verify, and adjust tax returns and related records: the Examination and Criminal Investigation Divisions. It is here that you can put up a fight about adjustments to your tax liability, if you know how. When the Examination Division calls you in to your local IRS office, more than likely a tax auditor will be waiting there for you. However, if a tax examiner calls on you at home or your place of business, he'll probably be a revenue agent.

If he's a *special* agent, he'll be investigating for possible criminal violations of Internal Revenue laws. That's why his division is so aptly named Criminal Investigation. Whereas tax auditors and revenue agents leave it to you to disprove their findings, the special agent's job is to prove you committed a crime. All three try to determine whether you filed your return improperly, then proceed to compute your correct tax liability, and may recommend penalties. Only in the case of special agents could the recommendation include criminal prosecution. Taxpayers who are worried about going to jail if their return is found deficient should know that prison is out of the Examination Division's domain. The possibility of a prison sentence normally enters the picture only after you've been investigated by a special agent from the Criminal Investigation Division.

The average taxpayer's chances of being investigated by a special agent are very slight: approximately ten thousand to one by nationwide statistics. There are only about twenty-five hundred special agents in the whole country, and each can usually handle no more than four cases per year—many of which are subsequently dropped. If an IRS criminal investigator ever does cross your path in the line of duty, more than likely it will be to obtain your testimony about another taxpayer under suspicion. While special agents interact with many more witnesses than suspects, most people will probably never be either.

No, if an IRS agent should become a temporary part of your life, chances are much greater that he will be an auditor or revenue agent from the Examination Division. Few of them are even remotely as sinister as many taxpayers seem to imagine. In fact, you may be surprised to learn how pleasant an audit can be, especially when you know what's going on and why. If you were ever in the Boy Scouts, you've already learned the key: Be Prepared. Then, unlike Benny Fischel, you need not worry about being made a fool of by the IRS—or by your perception of it.

Before you concern yourself with what the Internal Revenue Service can or cannot do to you, you ought to send them a tax return to sink their fangs into. Obviously, they can come after you if they suspect you failed to file, but the majority of examinations are triggered by something on a return that someone at IRS finds troublesome. There are dozens of books, including IRS Publication 17, that guide you in preparing tax forms; some claim they can help you prevent audits. This one will not attempt to duplicate

25

their comprehensive advice, but the following chapter may help you make the most fundamental decision of all—other than whether or not to file a return in the first place.

CHAPTER 2

To Itemize or Standardize

The whole messy business of taxation is just too much for some people to bother with. On top of thousands of pages of tax laws, amended tax laws, subsections, and appendices which we are all expected to obey—never mind if we understand them!—there are millions of pages of guidebooks, manuals, pamphlets, publications, and magazine articles constantly spilling forth from both government and private presses attempting to explain those original complicated tax laws. And then there are the armies of "economic wizards" competing for the right to advise you on how to decrease your tax bills, not to mention the politicians who keep coming up with clever new ways of saving government dollars—until they get elected, that is. The thought of all that tax information floating around is enough to give even a bureaucrat a neurosis. Isn't it possible to stay out of tax trouble without learning all that federal mumbo-jumbo?

In its finite wisdom, the government has devised something it is not accustomed to producing on a regular basis: an easy way out—at least for some of us. In one of its most merciful acts, it brought forth the *standard deduction,* for Americans who have no desire to wade through tax laws, or anything connected with tax laws. Standard deductions make life simpler not only for the persons taking them, but for the IRS that processes them. Imagine the ease of having to list only a few figures on your tax return: mainly, your W-2 salary, and the number of exemptions you're claiming, and your tax liability. Enclose your check if taxes are due, sign the return, mail it off, and in five minutes you've fulfilled your federal tax obligation. In many cases the IRS will even figure your tax liability for you. The standard deduction also saves you the trouble of keeping up with such annoying records as interest payments, contributions, medical expenses, and so on—all of those separate deductible expenditures which they considerately averaged together for you into one lump sum. What a marvelous invention!

There's one trouble with the standard deduction, if you possess that modicum of greed most people seem to have in their genes. Once you've taken it, there is that gnawing feeling that maybe you could have kept a few more of your hard-earned dollars in your own pocket had you itemized every legitimate deduction to which you were entitled. On the other hand, the standard deduction could turn out to be higher than all your legitimate itemized deductions put together, in which case you would lose money by itemizing. So what turned out to be an easy way out poses its own little stickler.

However, the problem is not insoluble. The easy way out of the easy way out requires a bit of calculation, but it's the only way you can be certain you're getting the best deal. Simply add together all the

deductions you're entitled to, which you can probably figure out by consulting a good tax-preparation booklet like Publication 17. If they total less than the standard deduction, you take the standard deduction. If they're higher, it's worth your while to itemize. Of course, if it's only a matter of a few dollars, you might just let it go—but by this time you've already gone to the trouble of computing all the figures, so it's not much extra trouble to transfer your figures to your tax return. In many of these borderline cases the difference winds up in your adviser's or return preparer's pocket anyway. So you've kept the government from it, but you didn't get much use out of it, either.

One way to handle the easy way out is to preplan your itemizing years. That is, decide in advance which year you are going to itemize, and plan to make enough deductible expenditures that year to exceed the standard deduction. (Make sure, before you proceed with your plans, that the government is not planning to raise it higher than your target figure.) You won't be making any more expenditures than you otherwise would have, it's just that you'll be timing them all to happen between January and December of your itemizing year.

For instance: Currently there are certain sales taxes you can deduct, in addition to the amounts listed in the IRS's prefigured sales-tax tables. Suppose you are planning to buy a new car next year. Here is one sales tax that will increase your deductions. Others include motor homes, sailboats, moving vans, and SST's. Buy any of these before your itemizing year is up, and hold onto the sales invoices, so you can

deduct all those sales taxes at the same time. The same goes for property taxes. Postpone paying your local government until just after the New Year rings in, but make up for your tardiness at the end of the same year by remitting the following year's payment in December. Then both payments can be deducted on one tax return. The more such itemized deductions you can double up on, the more likely you are to exceed the standard deduction. Now's the time to make that generous contribution to your favorite charity, and treat yourself to that biennial physical you've been putting off for five years. Any chance you see of making a deductible expenditure during your itemizing year, grab it! The more you can squeeze into one year, the more you're likely to save in taxes. Just be sure to save all the pertinent records, too, in case the IRS demands proof to back up all those deductions.

Planning an itemizing year takes some organization and foresight; you should be constantly on the alert for possible deductions, and you ought to keep up with any new deductions recently written into law. You should also keep all pertinent records—sales invoices, receipts from charities, doctor bills, and so on—filed in an accessible place. If they are not in a convenient place, you might just postpone that organizing chore until all your records are hopelessly jumbled together. One easy-to-get-to location could be your kitchen cabinets. Tape a few envelopes, labeled with each deduction category you're planning to take, inside a cabinet door; then just drop the receipts into the appropriate envelope as you obtain them. It's a

little extra work, but then, next year you plan to reward yourself—by taking the standard deduction.

One very nice feature of the standard deduction—you think—is that you won't be audited if you take it, since there is nothing the IRS can dispute, right? Wrong! Although the chances of being audited after taking a standard deduction *are* slim, they are not completely out of the picture. As Chapter 4 will explain, anyone can be selected for audit. Even if you had nothing to report but W-2 wages, you are not beyond the IRS's reach. But then, chances are the auditor will find nothing improper about your dull, run-of-the-mill tax return, and you'll be dismissed without having to make any changes whatever. However, even if you took the standard deduction, you may not be entirely safe. . . .

Aside from erroneously claiming such tax credits as insulation, or overstating business expenses, there's the problem of the faulty memory. Maybe you can't remember every little deposit, withdrawal, receipt, and source of income. To the best of your recollection, every deposit to your bank account was a paycheck, known to the IRS as "taxable income." But are you sure there wasn't something else that year, something that could have been nontaxable? One example: the U.S. Savings Bonds you cashed and then deposited. Bounced checks, refunds—anything you redeposited to your bank account, including your leftover vacation funds—may be added to your taxable total unless you can prove these deposits were not subject to taxation.

What about that three hundred dollars you loaned to good ol' George back in December 1977 to help him through the holidays? He repaid you in January 1978—three crisp new hundred-dollar bills—and you duly deposited them into your bank account without thinking any more about it. One year and three months later you list your usual W-2 wages and standard deduction on your 1978 tax return. Naturally you don't list the three-hundred dollar loan repayment, having already paid taxes on it the year in which you originally earned it, 1977. But then, in September 1980, a year and a half after you filed your 1978 return, it is audited.

Going over your bank's financial statement, the auditor notices that three-hundred-dollar deposit sticking out from the paycheck deposits like a sore elbow. And of course, like the thorough tax man he is, he asks you the source of this deposit, ever ready to add it to your taxable income total. Keep in mind, it's been two years and eight months since that January good ol' George repaid you—in cash—and he's never borrowed any money from you since. Do you think you'll remember that three hundred dollars as a nontaxable loan repayment after all that time? If you can't (and sometimes even if you can), the auditor may very well consider it unreported income, and you'll be charged an additional ninety dollars or so in tax and interest on money you've already paid taxes on.

There is a very simple way to avoid being taxed on the same money twice. For any bank deposit, especially an out-of-the-ordinary one, make a record of its source and hold on to it—particularly if it's nontaxable. A small notation on the deposit slip itself usually does fine—nothing fancy or poetic, just a simple "Repayment from George." Or you could enter it in your checkbook in close proximity to the space where you entered the amount of the deposit. Or if George signed an IOU, you could save a copy marked PAID and the date he repaid you. Just remember, your records should contain four key ingredients: the date, the amount, who gave you the money, and why.

But if you did not take these precautions, you might have to track George down and have him write a letter to the IRS affirming your claim that he did in fact borrow and repay that three hundred dollars on the dates you said he did. Good ol' George, he'll be glad to do that for you—if he's around, of course. But if George moved you-know-not-where a year ago, you might be stuck without a witness. Now your only way out of the tax is to hope the auditor believes you. He might, he might not, depending on his mood that day, how many other cock-and-bull stories he's been handed lately, and any number of other unrelated factors.

Another bank deposit that might slip your mind is your state-tax refund check. Of course, this could be easier to trace than a cash deposit, although the bank may charge a search fee. Generally, state-tax refunds are nontaxable for federal purposes, unless you itemized your "state taxes paid" on your previous year's return based on the figure listed on your W-2 form. If you got a refund from the state for that year, you deducted more than you actually owed, so that refund becomes taxable income to you in the year you receive it. If, however, you had figured the state taxes you owed first, and listed only that amount under "state taxes paid" on your federal return, the refund will be nontaxable. It would also be nontaxable if you had taken the standard deduction that year. But whether you itemize or take the standard deduction, it's a good idea to fully identify all deposits (especially nontaxable ones) so that if an auditor enters your life, he won't mistakenly try to tax nontaxable funds.

"Did you get a state-tax refund?" he might ask, trying to identify an irregular deposit to your bank account. His next question should then be: "Did you take the standard deduction on your previous return? If not, what did you deduct for state taxes on that return?" That will give him a clue as to whether or not to tax that unidentified deposit. And if he does not ask this last question, go ahead and answer it anyway.

"Do you deposit all of your income into your bank accounts?" he will ask. After your affirmative answer, he should also ask you what else you deposit besides paychecks, at which point you can display your recorded data for his wondering eyes to behold.

While your chances of being audited after taking the standard deduction are slight, it can happen—and you might even wind up being assessed for additional taxes. It's not something they bother with too much at the present time (less than one percent in 1979), but the day may come when the IRS will start cracking down more on these very ordinary tax returns. For years they have had a sneaking suspicion that W-2 wage-listers taking standard deductions really have more income than they're letting on. Many could be earning a little extra money on the side in what is known as "subterranean trade"—the kind of odd jobs that are not highly visible. [Nor is the income from such trades.] Sometimes they can uncover this practice during an audit of one of your customers, who states you insisted on being paid in cash—the harder for the IRS to find out about. Their next step: They come to you to verify your customer's statement, and that's when they learn about the little fix-it business you run in your spare time. In their callous disregard of the economic circumstances that forced you to supplement your wages, they snatch away from you part of the money that was supposed to make ends meet, and you're left with a pair of unmet ends.

It's taxpayers who itemize—do the long form—that consume the majority of the IRS's time and interest. If you're audited, they probably won't question every deduction claimed, but you're not likely to escape without at least one or two of them being challenged. Here again, written proof is your best defense. For instance, your contributions deduction seems out of proportion with your income. You politely explain that five hundred dollars of it was in the form of old clothes you donated to Goodwill. Then the auditor will want to know how you arrived at that value for them.

Like the Boy Scout who takes his motto seriously, you produce a detailed list of every item you donated, together with your estimate of a fair-market value for each (not as much as you originally paid, but perhaps more than you could get at a flea market). At the bottom is the signature of an authorized man of Goodwill acknowledging receipt of aforesaid items. The total value derived from the list: $500.25.

Very impressive. But let's say you get a rather nasty auditor, who won't even accept that list you took so much trouble to compile. Maybe you overestimated the value of those clothes, he decides. "How much do you think you could have gotten for them if you sold them at a garage sale?" he asks.

That you didn't expect. But if you think about it a second, what does it really have to do with the actual facts of the matter? You might point out—still politely, no need to start a ruckus—that people don't go to garage sales to pay fair market value for merchandise. They're there for bargains. So, you tell the auditor, that's not a fair comparison. It would be more proper to compare your deducted amounts with what you could have gotten if you owned a secondhand clothing store.

Not one to be put off, he might come back with a demand that you prove your original cost for those clothes. Now really, who saves all their department-store and boutique receipts, once they've decided not to return the merchandise? But he just wants to make sure before accepting them, that your estimates didn't exceed your costs. Even if he does end up knocking that five hundred dollars down a few pegs, he should give you some consideration. After all, giving half your family's wardrobe to charity is a very generous gesture. And what do they say about "He who gives . . . ?"

Miscellaneous deductions are another hot item—one of the grayest of gray areas, where people have listed everything from laundry bills to round-the-world cruises. The auditor will listen patiently to your explanation of why you claimed your new quadrophonic sound system as a deduction. "But I needed it to demonstrate music lessons to my first-graders!" you cry, launching into your best desperate interpretation of *HMS Pinafore*. But when he discovers you only take it to school two weeks a year, he may ask you to deduct a little from your deduction anyway, just to pay for his incredulity. Well, you knew you might have to compromise when you itemized it, so you don't argue too much. At least they let you keep the deduction for the casualty loss. You don't mention you were secretly glad when the thieves took that broken-down jalopy off your hands, which you couldn't have sold for half what you claimed it was worth. Of course, if they *had* questioned it, you were all ready to furnish the insurance records to corroborate your claim, weren't you?

It is not always necessary to provide written proof to back up your claims. If your return contained only a few questionable deductions totaling about fifty dollars, the auditor might just let it go, since it may not be worth the small additional tax he would compute making the change. Different audit groups have different "cutoff points," below which they usually won't bother to adjust. A certain degree of rationality goes into any audit. After all, the auditor is sure to realize that a businessman could not have made certain profits without incurring some expenses. If his claims for business expenses sound reasonable, although some may be undocumented, perhaps the auditor will allow them. Likewise, he might allow such other deductions as subscriptions to professional journals, church donations, and mileage expenses, for which no records may be available. But they won't believe everything—because they know they can't. That's why they so often demand documentation to prove you're telling the truth.

What about those "questionable" deductions you're not sure you're allowed to take? Many taxpayers go ahead and risk it, especially after they've been unable to find any reason for *not* claiming that "maybe" deduction in all the usual sources. If they're not challenged for the five hundred dollars worth of medical expenses or two thousand dollars Travel-and-Entertainment deduction, then it's theirs to keep. And if an auditor does try to disallow it, the taxpayer can ask to be shown where in the regulations that deduction is not allowed. Knowing the burden of proof is on the taxpayer, the auditor may not comply; but if enough doubt is created in his mind, he could look it up. Thanks to the taxpayer's persistence, the auditor might learn something he didn't know before.

If it can't be shown you are allowed that deduction, the auditor has every right to turn it into taxable income, and tax it at the going rate. However, if he tries to add a penalty for this oversight, that's worth fighting. If it happens to you, you might try this logic: "How could I have been negligent when I honestly tried to find out whether I could take that deduction? Nobody told me I couldn't until now, and I certainly didn't try to get away with it on *purpose!*" So you'll have to pay some extra tax; next time you'll know better. However, if the auditor disallows your "maybe" deduction without giving you a clear-cut reason, you might consider appealing to the Appellate Division (see Chapter 5).

* * *

The standard deduction has been a relief for tax-payers who don't want to bother with keeping track of deductible expenditures or struggling with a long, complicated tax return every April. But when your deductible total exceeds the standard deduction, it's probably worth your while to itemize. One way to do it is to plan itemizing years ahead of time, in which you consciously squeeze all your deductible expenditures together into one twelve-month period. Of course, be sure to keep records of everything you plan to deduct, in case you're audited. There have been instances when auditors have refused to recognize canceled checks as proof, suspecting the checks were simply exchanged for currency. But a tax man is generally more inclined to believe you if you have some documentation to support your claims, even if it's only a letter from a friend or associate. Taxpayers who itemize are more likely to be examined than those taking standard deduction, but the latter could also run into trouble if they can't identify non-income deposits to their bank accounts. So, even if you "standardize," you're not entirely safe.

Now that you are beginning to understand why it's so important to keep contemporaneous records for tax purposes, you need some idea of how long to keep them. Before you start compiling your entire financial history, read the next chapter.

CHAPTER 3

A Matter of Time

It couldn't have happened anywhere else in the world. Well, some of it could have, but what other country would admit it?

It all started when young Zero Gsryzunovitchski first set foot on American soil that gloomy night in 1959, determined to make something of himself, besides a nuisance. With only forty-four cents in his pocket and a fresh load of American soil clinging to his bare feet, he set off to seek his fortune. It had been a long haul from his native Outer Mongolia, where his eighteen sisters and brothers still languished in their tiny village of Inner Pietz. But Zero would not look back, not now, not when golden riches glittered on his horizon, just out of reach. It turned out to be his first encounter with a neon sign. "Smoke Luckies," it flashed, casting eerie halos round the smiling models and their fishing poles. To Zero, who knew little of smoking and less of luck, it was the sign he'd been hoping for: a prophecy, an omen promising wealth beyond his wildest dreams.

And indeed, it was with his original recipe for smoked guppies that Zero got lucky. It was in 1962 that he made his first million . . . and 1966 that he lost it. But by that time he had learned much about the ways of America and its wondrous system of taxation. With true Mongolian efficiency he spread his loss over the eight allowable years, back to 1963, the year he discovered Ed Sullivan, and forward to 1971, when he discovered adult bookstores. Even as his fortunes rose for the second time, Zero's taxes were being kept in check due to the Loss of 1966.

By the time Zero had discovered microwave ovens, sometime in 1975, he had made his second million, this time with psychedelic butterfly nets. The profits were so sudden and so huge, that the tax bite on them promised to be excruciating, compared to the moderate sums he'd been used to paying for the privilege of staying in his adopted country. But then Zero discovered income averaging, a means whereby he could spread his recent fortune out over five years, much as he had done with his loss, thereby reducing his tax liability. Zero felt very fortunate indeed to have discovered so hospitable a haven . . . until two years after he filed his '75 return, in 1978, when the Internal Revenue Service discovered Zero Gsryzunovitchski.

Just when Zero thought he had the system down pat, this strange tax man started asking him for records of his loss, dating back more than twelve years! But how could that be, when the statute of limitations is only three years?

"Well, you see," said the tax man, speaking slowly and distinctly, "you spread your loss up through 1971, which was one of the base years you used for income-averaging. And if that was wrong, then so was your

1975 return, you see? Now, think back to the year you lost your smoked-guppies business. . . ."

But the only figures that came to Zero's mind were the forty-four cents he had started out with (not taxable that year), and his two windfalls, the first of which was lost the year he discovered Haight-Ashbury. He had no records more than four years old with which to prove his claims. He became so hopelessly confused trying to reconstruct his financial history (having moved around a lot), that he longed for the simple life he'd left behind. It was the first time in years that anyone had actually asked for a visa to Outer Mongolia. . . .

The Internal Revenue Service has become a very suspicious lot over the years. Seldom will they take your word for fact, unless you can back it up with some sort of documentation. And even then they may have their doubts. Still, written words speak louder to the IRS than spoken ones, no matter how vociferously you shout. Will *you* be prepared when they ask you to prove a claim concerning transactions from several years in the past? You had the records *then*, all right, but what about now?

You never know when you might need an old financial record, nor *which* record might be called for. Realistically you can't save every scrap of your monetary history for a day that may never come. Then, too, unless you're superorganized, there would arise the problem of locating a specific record out of your cellarful of files. The experts suggest keeping pertinent ledgers, receipts, checks, statements, annotated checkbooks, deeds, and loan and sale records in labeled envelopes which you can get to easily. File cabinets are fine, too, as long as you *use* them.

But which records should go in them? The law requires you to keep adequate records, but never bothers to define precisely what it means by that. Those you do choose to retain, however, must be "permanent, accurate, and complete." Failure to keep records, when it is done deliberately and with evil intent, is a misdemeanor under Section 7203 of the Internal Revenue Code, punishable by up to one year in prison, ten thousand dollars in fines, or both, plus cost of prosecution. You certainly don't want that to happen to you, just because you threw away the wrong papers. If you must dispose of some of your records before the statutes expire, for whatever reason, it may be better to start with taxable-income records. Do hang on to those expense and nontaxable-income records, though, such as loan proceeds, loans repaid to you, gifts, inheritances, and so forth. Then, if you're audited, at least you'll still be able to prove your deductions and nontaxable income.

Once you figure out which records to keep, how long should you keep them? The general IRS rule is: three years from the date the tax return was due or filed, whichever is later; or two years from the date you paid your taxes, if that is later. Employers should retain withholding-tax records for four years after paying them.

Normally the statute of limitations for civil tax purposes is three years. It's also three years for cases of wilful failure to keep records (Section 7203 above), and failure to file an information return. This simply means that they have three years from the date your return was due or filed (whichever is later) to make adjustments on it. However, it doesn't mean they will wait all that long to initiate action. They like to give themselves as much time as they think may be necessary to make a thorough examination of your return allowing for any reasonable delays or procrastination on your part. That's why many districts normally won't bother with returns that are more than thirty months old. Legally, of course, they could take the full three years to contact you. If it has been more than three years since you dodged your taxes, they probably can't collect them now. However, there are several notable exceptions to the three-year limit:

1) If an understatement of income involved represents twenty-five percent or more of gross income, the civil statute of limitations is six years.

2) For civil fraud, there is no time limit.

3) In cases of civil failure to file a tax return, again—no limit. However, for criminal prosecution for failure to file, the statute is six years.

The same six-year limit goes for these other criminal violations:

4) Wilful attempt to defeat or evade tax.

5) Wilfully aiding or assisting in the preparation of false returns or other documents.

6) Wilful failure to pay tax or make return.

7) Wilfully filing false return.

8) Wilfully submitting false documents.

9) Forcible attempt to interfere with the administration of Internal Revenue laws.

10) Conspiracy in connection with tax evasion.

Submitting false documents under Section 1001, Title 18 of the U.S. Code has a statute of limitations of five years.

These are the more common statutes. There are other specific civil statutes, ranging from a seven-year limit for claiming bad debts to Section 6503 (f) of the Tax Code, "Extensions of Time for Payment of Tax Attributable to Recoveries of Foreign Expropriation Losses"; and some of these are very much open to interpretation. If your situation does not fit the more common statutes and you're not sure whether your time has run out, check with a competent accountant or a good tax attorney, or ask the IRS (anonymously if you prefer).

If you have records pertaining to any of the above activities, now you know how long to keep them. Of course, you would never be guilty of any of those sins . . . but what if they *accuse* you of committing them? That's why you need to save those records. In general the IRS likes to tell taxpayers to retain their records "as long as their contents are material to the administration of any Internal Revenue law." Very helpful. You could have figured that out for yourself.

What about copies of your old tax returns? Should you follow the lead of the IRS, and destroy them after seven years? They would be very grateful if you did hang on to them at least that long, especially if they themselves can't find your original returns when they ask you in for an audit. But suppose you also lost track of a particular return? It's not your fault the IRS lost the original you sent them, and no law specifically states that you have to retain your copy.

So, no original—no copy—no way to verify it or make adjustments. Oh, they could get a little information from their gargantuan computer: the fact that you did file, and perhaps your taxable income reported, the amount of taxes paid, a few totals—but not the entire return. They might request a complete set of your books to reconstruct the return. But if those records are not so complete chances are they'll just accept the return as filed—wherever it is.

You might take your copy along when you head for the audit, if you happen to have it handy; but if they don't know you have it, how can they make you produce it, just because they can't find your original? One fellow managed to "lose" the only available copy of his tax return after his auditor excused himself for what turned out to be more than a little while, right in the middle of the audit. When he finally returned to his desk—no taxpayer, and no tax return. The taxpayer swore he didn't know what happened to the return they'd been working on. All he had to say was that with the auditor gone that long, he figured the auditor had finished with him. Besides, he had other things to do with his time. Of course, if they could prove he had stolen that tax return, they could charge him with a felony.

Some records cry out to be retained longer than others. One obvious example is anything pertaining to your assets, which you might conceivably sell some day. Later on, if you can prove your costs, the IRS may not allow you to deduct your actual cost from the final sale price. Instead, they can assume a cost they think is reasonable and base your tax on what may be a higher figure. Of course, if you have been deferring gains from asset to progressively larger and costlier asset, your cost basis for your latest asset must be traced back to the first one. For instance, the house you bought for $20,000 sold for $40,000, which you put right back into a new house costing $40,000. That subsequently sold for $80,000, with which you bought another house for $80,000. You sell that for $120,000. Now, what are your profits? $40,000? Try again. If you have been deferring your gains from taxation all this time, your gain is $100,000; the difference between the final sale price and your original $20,000 investment. Of course, if you have lost some of your records during all that moving, it could wind up as a guessing game.

Generally you should retain records of your assets, beginning with your receipt for their purchase, for at least three years after you sell them, beginning with April 15th of the following year. This is particularly true when inflation is on the rampage. The dollars may be worth less, but if you get more of them for an asset than you paid, that constitutes a profit—at least on paper.

If one or more of your valuable assets are stolen, you may be able to claim their value as a casualty loss. However, just as insurance companies request proof that you actually owned the stolen merchandise, so may the IRS if they are to allow the deduction: another good reason for hanging on to those records, whether they're in the form of a sales receipt or a police report. And what about time payments—installment, or deferred-payment sales? Again, you should keep those records at least until three years after all monies have been collected.

Bad debts are like assets when it comes to substantiating a deduction. Once you've deemed it uncollectible and written it off as a legitimate tax deduction, don't make the mistake of throwing the unpaid note away. It may be the only proof you'll be able to offer an auditor when he asks for an explanation; but that in itself may not be enough. Before you can declare a debt bad, you should have attempted to collect it, and he may also ask for proof of that, such as a copy of a certified letter containing your bill. Then, too, if the debt should eventually be repaid, your copy of the note marked PAID will identify the corresponding deposit to your bank account as a loan repayment and explain why you didn't include this nontaxable income on your tax return (assuming you had not deducted it as yet).

There are certain unusual records that should be retained for a long, long time; not only to entertain future historians, but just in case you ever find yourself in a situation like that of our friend Zero from Outer Mongolia. Whenever you spread a loss out over several years for tax purposes, it can affect tax returns for years to come. So any papers having to do with losses should become part of your permanent records. Also remember, if you income-average, every record that can affect a base-year computation should be retained until you are satisfied the statute has expired for the year you averaged your income. If Zero had only kept such records on hand, he might still be living in America, working on his third fortune.

Spreading out losses or sudden large profits for tax purposes has become a time-honored tradition among certain alert taxpayers. This book will not attempt to describe these methods in detail, since the IRS will gladly supply you with free publications containing step-by-step instructions, should you ever feel the urge to income-average, as Zero did. These booklets are especially helpful to people whose fortunes tend to rise and fall as if their income scale were a seesaw.

Let's take a closer look at Zero's case, and see why the tax man was so interested in his loss records twelve years after the fact. When he lost his first million in 1966, he spread the loss over eight years, starting three years earlier and ending in 1971. This negated almost all of his taxable income for those years, affording him refunds for the three previous years, and nothing to pay taxes on through 1971.

After the five-year carry-forward was up, Zero started paying his regular taxes again, entering a higher tax bracket each year, until his windfall of 1975. To ease his tax bite, he averaged that year's income back over the previous four years, reducing the total taxes he would have had to pay if taxed at the regular rate. Everything was fine until 1978, when the IRS decided to audit Zero's 1975 return, nine months before the statute of limitations was due to expire for that year.

Since 1971 was the fourth year of Zero's income-averaged base period, the accuracy or inaccuracy of that 1971 return would affect the tax due for 1975 on the income-averaging form. The auditor knew the law: "You are required to use correct taxable income for each base-period year, whether or not the assessment of a deficiency . . . for this base-period year is barred by the statute of limitations." In other words, if the 1971 return turned out to be wrong, the IRS

49

probably wouldn't assess taxes on it, but it could cause a chain reaction right through the 1975 return—the one being audited. In 1971 Zero was still deducting his Loss of 1966, leaving him zero taxable income. Zero explained this to the auditor, who promptly demanded proof of that loss. That's when Zero first started thinking wistfully of home.

"Can't you just go back to your own files and check?" he asked hopefully.

"The only records we would have are your tax returns, and any over seven years old are long gone. Anyway, a return by itself wouldn't prove you had a loss. Surely you must have *some* documentation proving you had a loss that year."

"Surely, surely," Zero agreed. "But not anymore. It helped get me through tough years, but it's not something I wanna brag to my friends. All records were destroyed, so I don't have nothing to remind me of bad times. How could I know I need them again?"

Poor Zero. Even poorer than he thought, when the auditor disallowed the income-averaging because Zero couldn't prove the loss carry-forward, increasing his 1975 tax liability by twenty thousand dollars. To be sure, he was still left with a sizeable portion of his second fortune, but the curious practices of the IRS had soured him on America, or anything American. Life in Mongolia may have been hard, he thought (in Mongolian), but at least it was simpler.

Well, it could have been worse. Had criminal action been taken, the statute for 1975 would have expired in 1982—sixteen years after the loss! Even later if Zero had filed his 1975 return late. Remember, the statute starts running when the return is filed if it's later than the date it was due.

Moral: For any irregular tax return, such as loss carry-backs and income-averaging, always retain some record of it—including every year that was or will be affected by it—until all statutes of limitations on all years affected have passed.

You may think some people get away with tax crimes just by being patient long enough to outlast the statute of limitations. You're right, *but* . . . sometimes it's possible to catch one of these unsavory characters after, say, a six-year statute has run out. If circumstances warrant, the Justice Department can suspend the running time, or extend it. The process is called "tolling," but it has nothing to do with bells or highway fees. If, for example, the grand jury is not in session when a U.S. attorney was planning to seek an indictment against a taxpayer, and the sixth anniversary of his offense would pass before the grand jury reconvened, the attorney can file a "complaint" with a U.S. commissioner showing probable cause that the offense was indeed committed. The commissioner may then "toll" the statute, that is, suspend it until the charges can be brought before the grand jury and the resulting trial concluded.

Sometimes it can actually be to your advantage to extend voluntarily the statute of limitations. Why would you want to give the IRS even more time to haunt you? Because at times, when they know the statute is about to expire, they'll try to hurry their work along so they can still assess you for additional taxes. In their haste they may overlook some legitimate deductions, or just disallow everything in one fell swoop. In this case you might then be assessed a greater amount of additional taxes than you rightfully owe. You could still contest them later on, and present all sorts of documentation to support your claims. But you might have saved yourself the trouble had you given them the extra time they needed to figure your taxes correctly. However, if you are under criminal investigation, it could be better not to voluntarily extend the statute. Under current IRS policy any forced civil settlements arrived at before the investigation is over can hamper criminal recommendations for that year. If they are not forced to come up with a quick settlement, the way is cleared for a criminal investigation, which can last a long time. Now, if the criminal investigator can't find enough intent to indicate fraud for that particular year, the civil aspects of the case can still be carried on, because the accommodating taxpayer consented to extend the normal three-year statute of limitations.

Other situations in which the statute may be extended are: 1) if the taxpayer is a fugitive from justice, or 2) the taxpayer is outside the United States. For Zero Gsryzunovitchski, time has stood still. Before IRS could collect the twenty thousand dollars they'd assessed, a frustrated Zero had caught the next freighter bound for home. His case was tolled until he returns from Outer Mongolia—something he swears he'll never do.

How long should you keep financial records? According to the IRS, "as long as their contents are material to the administration of Internal Revenue laws." This usually means until the statute of limitations expires; however, if no return was filed or civil fraud was involved, there is no time limit for civil purposes. For the majority of civil cases, however, the statute is three years from the date your return was due or filed, whichever is later, or two years from the date you paid your taxes, if that is later. Criminal tax violations usually carry a six-year statute of limitations, which is one reason some IRS experts advise holding onto records for six years, to guard against unforeseen events. Your retained records may help prove your innocence.

Some records should be retained much longer. These include documents pertaining to purchase and sale of assets, installment or deferred payments, bad debts, and especially irregular tax returns such as those that were income-averaged or contained loss carry-overs. Old tax returns are kept by the IRS for seven years, but no law says you must do likewise. The law does require you to keep records that are "permanent, accurate, and complete," but does not specify precisely which records should be retained. Once you've made your choices, based on the income, exemptions, and deductions you list on your tax return, you can breathe easier. You are now ready for whatever the IRS asks of you—such as your presence at an audit.

CHAPTER 4

They'd Audit Their Own Grandmothers!

It's not the most pleasant experience in the world, but worse things can happen to you. Some are seized with guilt and fear, some with nervousness, and some with hay fever, when they've learned they've been summoned. It's not the sort of thing you plan for, but it's not exactly like being hit by a meteor from out of the blue, either. It's more like getting called by the Gallup poll: It happens to any number of people every day, and sooner or later they could pull your name out of their monstrous hat. It is entirely possible to live through your entire life without being audited by the IRS—a not disagreeable prospect—but there is no shame in being among the chosen many who are invited to open their books to an Internal Revenue Servant. To estimate your chances of being audited, see the accompanying statistics. If your number does come up, at least you have the satisfaction of knowing that your government is taking an interest in you. Whatever comfort that might be. . . .

The government seems to take more of an interest in some taxpayers than they do in others. Willy Ketchup has received an invitation to an audit eight years in a row, almost like clockwork. He'd just as

Returns filed, Examination Coverage: This table contains break-downs of the types of returns audited in 1979.

	Returns Filed	Total Returns Examined	Percent Coverage	Percent With No Change
Individual, Total	87,338,611	1,844,986	2.11	23*
Form 1040—Standard	28,749,451	191,986	.67	28*
Nonbusiness under $10,000—Itemized	10,147,045	253,586	2.50	26*
Nonbusiness $10,000–$15,000	12,627,936	284,585	2.25	24*
Nonbusiness $15,000–$50,000	24,227,838	704,024	2.91	23*
Nonbusiness $50,000 and over	966,659	101,989	10.55	26*
Business Under $10,000	4,043,915	132,617	3.28	20*
Business $10,000–$30,000	5,132,040	92,933	1.81	17*
Business $30,000 and over	1,443,728	83,266	5.77	16*
Fiduciary	1,744,478	10,170	.58	34
Form 1065 Partnership	1,195,186	30,474	2.55	44
Corporation, Total	1,920,371	142,937	7.44	25
Assets Not Reported	123,526	8,280	6.70	31
Under $100,000	959,614	40,178	4.19	32
$100,000–$1 million	674,357	53,520	7.94	25
$1 million–$10 million	133,719	28,629	21.41	19
$10 million–$100 million	24,421	8,373	34.29	11
$100 million and over	4,734	3,957	83.59	4
Small Business Corporation	444,860	11,523	2.59	39
Disc Corporation	7,776	1,435	18.45	37
Estate, Total	158,045	29,232	18.50	12
Gross Estate Under $300,000	122,330	12,741	10.42	14
Gross Estate $300,000 and over	35,715	16,491	46.17	10
Gift	194,848	11,723	6.02	21
Excise	881,554	82,104	9.31	21
Employment	25,592,993	109,019	.43	32

* Calculated using actual percent for revenue agents and tax auditors and overall no change percentage for service centers.

—From the 1979 IRS Commissioner's Report

soon the government turned its attention on somebody else for a change—maybe his neighbor, Jake Crabgrass, who is beginning to feel left out. Jake has never been audited in all the forty years he's been paying taxes—although he did get a letter from them one year because he had a $1.97 math error on his return. Other than that, they don't seem to know Jake exists. Willy, on the other hand, has become one of the "regulars." Maybe they just like him around the IRS office.

Like Willy, you, too, might wonder, "Why me?" even if you've been audited only once. You may have filed your tax return a month before the deadline every year, usually taking the standard deduction; your payments have gone through without a hitch, and you can't think of a single thing that could have been wrong. And maybe that's just what the audit will show. It's not only the tax cheaters who are audited—although the IRS likes to pull in as many of them as they can—*anyone* can be called for an audit. They do it to presidents, after all—why not you? Nobody can accuse the IRS of discrimination.

Basically there are six ways your number can pop up on the audit roster. They can get you through:

1) the Discriminate Function System which compares your return with national averages;

2) a random sampling for the Taxpayer Compliance Measurement Program;

3) matching information documents (1099's, partnership returns, etc.) to your return;

4) a target-group project;

5) noticing an obvious discrepancy on your tax return; or

6) tips from informants.

Sometimes an individual IRS employee may suggest a person for an audit if, through his own observation, he suspects that person of cheating on taxes. But let's stick with the more usual procedures.

The *DIF* (Discriminate Function System) is a set of mathematical formulas devised by IRS statisticians to establish the average taxes paid and deductions taken by each income bracket. The tables are adjusted periodically to keep pace with economic conditions. They start with a cross-section of income brackets for individuals and businesses, which is available in abundance in the tax-return files, and elsewhere. This data is averaged together to produce "weighted averages," for deductions for each income bracket. For instance, if your income is twenty thousand dollars and you list contributions totaling ten thousand dollars, it's a sure bet your return won't conform to the weighted averages. Perhaps one of your tax returns was used to establish a weighted average—but you may never know if it was or wasn't. If it was, you may have helped set a standard without even realizing it. And they didn't even send you a thank-you note.

Once these weighted averages have been determined, they're programed into the IRS's mammoth computer, which proceeds to compare each tax return fed into it with the acceptable deductions. Any deduction that is greater than the weighted averages is given a

DIF score: the more it deviates from the "norm," the higher its score. The computer then adds the deduction scores together to produce a total DIF score for that return. Those returns that exceed a predetermined level are spit back out for possible auditing. But even that doesn't mean they *will* be audited; the fact that a return has a high DIF score may have any number of legitimate explanations—which is why an IRS employee, perhaps a return classifier or a group manager, will personally check each return singled out by the computer before recommending it for audit. Sometimes the reason the return did not match the weighted averages becomes readily apparent at that point. For instance, the return classifier might notice you sold some rental property at a loss, which would explain the discrepancy. That's something the computer may not have been programed to understand.

The DIF program was devised to increase the odds of catching discrepancies. Since its implementation in 1969, according to the 1978 commissioner's report, examinations resulting in no tax change dropped from forty-two to twenty-four percent. As long as the IRS are taking it upon themselves to examine tax returns, they'd rather find as many as they can that owe additional tax. Otherwise they could waste a lot of taxpayer-supported time finding nothing but perfect tax returns. Of course, DIF scores are only numbers, and can't guarantee each unmatched return will be out of order; neither will the personnel who eliminate some and assign others to be audited—they're only human, after all. But this method does yield a higher percentage of improprieties than would just pulling names out of the hopper at random. The IRS has a computer program that does play that game, but for a slightly different purpose.

The computer-selected *random sample* is called the Taxpayer Compliance Measurement Program. TCMP, as it's abbreviated, selects a random cross-section of various classes of taxpayers: individuals earning ten thousand to twenty-five thousand dollars, corporations reporting more than a million, and so on. This TCMP data is used for research data and also to update DIF scores. Whereas the much larger DIF program explicitly seeks out as many errors as possible, the TCMP concerns itself primarily with representative categories of taxpayers from different classes, just to reassure the IRS that people are voluntarily filing their returns and paying their taxes. Of course, when they discover about five billion dollars worth of unpaid taxes in a single year, their already shaky faith in basic American honesty once again falters, and their justification to keep examining taxpayers is strengthened.

If during your audit you happen to notice the letters TCMP stamped in the corner of your tax return—and that it's being scrutinized by a rather unhappy-looking auditor—congratulations! Your return has been singled out to pose as a "model" against which others will be measured. Out of millions of possibilities, your tax return was chosen to help set a standard. Lucky you. Now you'll get to spend more than twice as long as you would at an ordinary audit patiently justifying every little deduction, exemption, and calculation. Of course, if adjustments are in order, these will be duly entered before your return goes on to fame and stardom.

Recently the IRS, with the help of its supercomputer, has devised a new system that increases the possibilities of catching unreported income. It has to do with those little information slips that begin changing hands as filing season draws near. These include things like W-2 forms, on which your employer reports your wages and withheld taxes; 1099's, which your savings bank sends you so you'll know how much interest income to report; and partnership returns. The new system has greatly expedited a once time-consuming process. According to the 1979 IRS Commissioner's Report, they expect, in the near future, to match about eighty percent of the information returns to individuals' tax returns, just to see if the information on the former is being properly reported on the latter. If, for instance, the computer discovers you neglected to report the interest recorded on the 1099 sent in by your bank, you might find yourself trying to explain this discrepancy to an auditor. And how often do you suppose they'll swallow the "must-have-been-lost-in-the-mail" excuse?

Being part of a target-group *project* is something else again. Now the IRS is really getting picky with their pickings. They have decided to scrutinize the returns of a minimum number of people from a targeted group that may have a high probability of discrepancies. A certain professional group (doctors, lawyers, etc.) may be selected because it could be easy for its members to hide income. It's not that these people would necessarily have a greater propensity to cheat on their taxes than members of other groups; but they do have a greater opportunity to do so than average W-2 salaried employees, for instance. So the IRS pulls out all the returns filed by, say, disco owners earning at least fifty thousand dollars, and any that appear irregular will be called in for an audit. If they're really irregular, a special agent may be assigned to the case to investigate for possible criminal violations. Or maybe they'll just call in every disco owner in the district, regardless of their income, whether irregularities are suspected or not.

In some projects they look for specific violations. For example, they might decide to audit plumbers in certain areas if they are suspected of making extra money on the side and not reporting it. Conditions in the marketplace have led the IRS to focus their attention on those overnight opportunists likely to be cashing in on new consumer demands. When the furniture industry was booming, for instance, lumber producers in some areas were reaping a bonanza in profits; the IRS thus audited a large percentage of them, to keep them as honest as they had been during leaner years.

The IRS is constantly on the lookout for evasion schemes, and will go after the most likely suspects, based on current events and patterns emerging from previous audits. Partnerships in high-loss categories (twenty-five thousand or more) have been the subject of increased IRS interest, since they've discovered rather shady dealings taking place in some of them. The discovery of deficiencies in one partner's return has led to an audit of the partnership return. If one partner understated his income, it could be the partnership return was incorrect; in that case the IRS may assume there will be corresponding deficiencies in the individual returns of the other partners.

But it doesn't have to be a partner's tax return that will lead a tax man to someone else's. During an audit one individual could tell an agent he paid another individual in cash; the auditor might later check up on that person who demanded cash, to make sure those payments were reported on his tax return. On the other side of the IRS target are companies in certain regulated industries, like oil, motion pictures, and real estate. You may have read about their antics, uncovered by IRS, in the newspaper.

Very often it's a *discrepancy* on the tax return itself that can trigger IRS action. For instance, you may have otherwise fallen into a category with less than a three percent chance of being audited, except that you claimed forty-eight exemptions. That being the case, your chances increase substantially.

The computer does not automatically pinpoint drastic changes that occur on your return from one year to the next. But once in a while the IRS will run a program designed to locate returns with specific changes on them. A sharp decrease in reported income or sudden increase in interest income does not necessarily indicate wrongdoing, but it may very well arouse suspicion to the point of causing you to be brought in to explain your return. And indeed, you may have a very good explanation: you lost all your customers to a tax-exempt church that started competing with you at bargain prices; or the bottom fell out of your underwear market and you almost lost your T-shirt. If you get a particularly sympathetic auditor, maybe he will even shed a tear as he marks "accepted as filed" on your return. Just don't offer him your monogrammed silk hanky and ask him to help carry your records back to your custom-built Cadillac. This could give you away almost as surely as an informant's tip.

Of course, you'd rather not have anybody *inform* on you to the IRS. But if they do get a "squeal letter" or telephone tip implying your tax return was not what it should be, you might just hear from them—if they deem the information worth following up. If it's really damaging, the case could go right to a criminal investigator. Of course, who's going to tattle on you? Your financial affairs are all in order . . . aren't they?

Informants, discrepancies, projects, information return-matching, random samplings, and DIF scores— these are the six most common ways you can be selected for an audit. Not that it matters how they picked you, though, once your presence has been requested. Auditors generally won't tell you why your return was selected, as they'll be too busy asking you about your income, deductions, expenditures, and so forth. The auditor may not even know himself why they picked you; he just examines what's assigned to him—a new one every half hour or so.

You might approach an IRS audit with roughly the same kind of trepidation you used to feel as a child when your mother found your greasy fingerprints on her cookie jar. Actually, you'd be surprised how friendly examiners can be. In fact, they take as much interest in you personally as they do in your books and records. Not only does it make for a more pleasant audit, but in so relaxed an atmosphere, you're likely to talk more freely about things that have a bearing on your taxes—things the auditor will be listening very intently for—things you might have kept to yourself if the auditor had come on like the Grand Inquisitor. Many substantial changes can often be traced back to the horse's big mouth, opened by an affable auditor. So, if you're a talkative type inclined to take a few liberties on your tax return, maybe you do have reason to be a little apprehensive about being audited.

On the other hand, if the auditor—or any tax man, for that matter—makes the Marquis de Sade look like a Teddy bear, there is someone to whom you can complain about the abuse. Whenever you feel an IRS agent has harassed you, you can report him directly to his group manager, who should take appropriate action; or you may report him to the IRS Internal Security Division, which is the IRS's way of policing itself. Tax men enjoy having one of these inspectors on their tails about as much as taxpayers enjoy being investigated by IRS. So if a tax man gets too offensive, reporting him—or threatening to report him—to the Internal Security Division is a way to retaliate. (By the way, if you abuse a tax man, he has the same option.)

How well you come out of the audit depends partly on your own behavior. Taxpayers have arrived with all sorts of preconceived notions about how to treat the auditor. Some come on like an old buddy from way back, hoping their warm greetings and suffocating bear hug will ingratiate them with "my good friend, the tax man. What would America do without you, buddy boy?" The tax man will probably not be amused. Sure, he's human, he likes being treated kindly as much as anybody else. But on the job he considers himself a professional, and conducts himself accordingly. He expects the same kind of businesslike attitude from you.

In contrast to the "buddy-buddy" approach, don't storm into an IRS office with a chip on your shoulder, ready to hurl it into the auditor's face. As much as you may resent taking time out of your busy schedule to show your perfectly filled-out tax return to an IRS snoop, try not to take it out on the auditor. He's there to do a job, and if you start making it harder for him, he may be inclined to retaliate. If he looks hard enough, he can usually find something to disallow; whereas, if you simply follow the dictates of common courtesy, he'll probably keep down "the heat" he can so deftly apply.

There are a couple of other types of taxpayers who don't arouse an auditor's sympathy, either. One is the supplicant, who comes in overflowing with apologies for the mistake he knows he made. Watch out, you would-be repentants! Now the auditor will most likely examine your return even more closely than usual. Your meek confession, "I know now what I did wrong," alerts him to the possibility that you may be trying to divert him from other little "mistakes" by calling attention to just one. And he'll be looking for them.

"I knew you'd catch up to me sooner or later," some good-natured taxpayers will blurt out upon entering an audit. Not a good idea, even if you meant it in jest. Many auditors do have a sense of humor, we hasten to point out, but that's one "joke" you shouldn't tell. To a tax man, it's just another warning signal. Why not try the one about the traveling salesman and the farmer's daughter?

Keep in mind that an IRS audit could be the first step leading to an even more intensive investigation of you, if enough wrongdoing is suspected. If you have nothing at all to hide, confident your tax return was correct as filed, all well and good. But if you're guilty and you know it, tread carefully. The IRS may not catch all unreported income or overstated deductions, but they look nevertheless. If some of it shows up on your return, it might be a good idea to admit frankly your "temporary oversight" when the auditor catches it. It's certainly better than trying to lie your way out of trouble, which could wind up having the opposite effect: if they later do start a criminal investigation on you, those little fibs you told the auditor could be used against you in court.

Usually you won't be able to tell at the audit if they plan to take any criminal action against you—or further civil action, for that matter. But if you should learn that they have ordered one of your previous (or subsequent) tax returns to be examined, the odds are they suspect something out of the ordinary. Face it, they didn't order that second return just because they wanted some light reading for their lunch hour. It does not guarantee you will become the subject of a criminal investigation—even if they do find something wrong on the second return—but the chances are slightly higher.

Whether your return was chosen via electronic or human agency, it will pass through at least one pair of human hands before it is refiled or assigned to an auditor. It is at this juncture that, with a little foresight, you might have saved yourself some trouble, by action you could have taken when you mailed in the return. If the decision-maker spots an irregularity on your return which may call for an explanation from you, an audit may be the logical course. However, if you had the foresight to enclose the explanation with your return, that may be all that is necessary to clear up any doubts. For instance, if you deducted an inordinately large amount of sales taxes, the reason could lie in several major purchases you made during that particular year. Enclose a copy of the sales contract from Geronimo's Pierce Arrow Sales with a highly noticeable circle drawn round the sales-tax figure, and you could save yourself a trip to the IRS office. It might even spare you the annoyance of having to answer additional unrelated questions the auditor could have thrown in as long as you were in his presence such as, "By the way, is Fido your natural child, or did you adopt him?" As long as your attached documentation passes snuff, they may just pass you up when it comes to sending out those summonses to audits.*

Some taxpayers have actually had the gall to refuse

---

*Caution: If you attach too many explanatory documents to your return, you can wind up being audited—because the return classifier won't have time to go over more than a few. So, keep them to a minimum.

their neatly printed invitations. The IRS frowns upon this sort of thing. Ignore your boss's birthday party, if you like, or your semiannual dentist visit, even your niece's first ballet recital—but an audit by the IRS? That is not considered good form. If it's just the appointment time you find inconvenient, simply call the IRS office and ask them to reschedule you. But if you're trying to get out of being found out, you could just intensify your troubles by being obstinate. Ignore their letters and phone calls long enough, and they might adjust your return based on whatever they have on you, without giving you a chance to defend yourself. They may disallow every deduction you claimed, even the legitimate ones, and raise your taxes accordingly. A revenue officer may then be sent to collect them, or they might withhold the amount due from a subsequent refund check you were expecting. They may even send a special agent from the Criminal Investigation Division to visit you, to find out how deceitful you really are. At that point you may have wished you'd kept your appointment with the auditor.

Remember, just because you've been selected for an audit by the IRS does not necessarily mean you did something wrong. They do try to pull in as many returns with discrepancies as they can find, but in quite a few cases it turns out that no additional tax is owed. And sometimes the lucky taxpayer who entered the audit all worried he'd be found deficient comes back out as happy as the beachcomber who's stumbled upon an old treasure chest—because all they've discovered is that he's due a refund. He never would have gotten it if he hadn't gone to the audit. Now he hopes they'll call him again.

Once a tax examiner has made up his mind to disallow a deduction it can be very difficult to get him to change it. It's not that they're stubborn necessarily; it's just that if they believed everything everyone told them, the national treasury would be even deeper in debt than it already is. Also, imagine if an IRS agent never collected additional taxes; he might begin to wonder if he's really needed. His bosses might, too. Of course, taxpayers never thought he was needed in the first place.

CHAPTER 5

The Appeal of Negligence, and Other Penalties

Not every tax return that is examined by the IRS will be found deficient, but those that are will usually be assessed for more than just additional taxes owed. At the very least they will add interest charges for each month, beginning with that spring day when the taxes were due. Like the prime rate, IRS interest rates change regularly, but are usually lower than the prime rate. Your local IRS office can tell you what the current rates are. However, before you take it upon yourself to "borrow" money from the IRS at their lower rates by claiming disallowable deductions, consider this: If they audit you, you may have to remit not only any additional taxes due plus interest, but possibly civil penalties as well. Even if these total less than the interest rate you would have had to pay someone else, only the interest portion is deductible on your next tax return—not the penalties. Had you borrowed that money from an official lender, you could have deducted all of the interest for that loan.

The civil penalties IRS can tack onto the average taxpayer's bill range from as low as five tenths of a percent (.5%) per month for failure to timely pay tax, to two hundred percent (that's *two hundred per*

70

cent!) for claiming excessive credits for gasoline and oil for business nonhighway use. There are more than a dozen little-used penalties in between and one is even higher—three hundred percent. Civil penalties can be recommended by the auditor or revenue agent acting alone, without anyone else's approval. When considering the harsher penalties, though, he may consult his group manager or a review staff, especially in borderline cases. In fact, a review staff may recommend a penalty despite the auditor's initial decision against it. After all, the auditor might be inclined toward leniency under the influence of your winning personality, but a review staff knows you only by your tax records, which are about as personable as pabulum. When the penalty under consideration is for civil fraud, tax examiners may seek the advice of a special agent.

More than twenty million civil penalties were assessed by the IRS in 1979, amounting to $1.8 billion. That same year $383.7 million worth of penalties were removed, or, as the IRS calls it, abated. Among the more commonly assessed civil penalties against individuals are the following:

1) Failure to pay estimated tax: one percent of the underpaid amount per month, up from one half of one percent per month effective February 1980. For each quarter of unpaid estimated tax, the penalty will be in effect until the yearly return is due (such as April 15 of the following year), at which point the failure-to-file and failure-to-pay penalties may begin. The taxpayers who expect to owe at least one hundred dollars in taxes not accounted for on W-2 forms, and

meet certain other conditions (these are spelled out in IRS Publications 17 and 505), are required to predict how much they expect to earn each year, and pay taxes on this money during the year. In 1979 more than three million estimated-tax payers turned out to be inept prophets of profits, and were duly penalized for their faulty forecasts, to the tune of more than $212 million.

The IRS has yet to admit that the fault could lie with their future-dependent regulations, insisting that taxpayers should have no trouble figuring out in advance how much they're going to make. Rather than allow people to pay taxes on money they're sure they've earned after the fact, the bureau just continues printing up millions of "Underpayment of Estimated Tax" forms, which contain step-by-step instructions on how to calculate your own penalty. (Form 2210—for individuals—and Form 2210F—for farmers and fishermen—also list exceptions to the penalty.)

If you estimate your tax liability and come within eighty percent of being correct, you're usually all right. They don't expect your prediction to be right on the nose. And if you should *over*pay your estimated tax, you can either use the excess as a credit toward the next quarter, or file for a refund at the end of the year. If, as the quarter proceeds, you discover your estimates and payments were not high enough and you fear you'll have to pay the penalty, you may be able to save yourself by filing an amended Form 1040-ES. The IRS allows one amended form per quarter. The whole complicated procedures to be exempted from the penalty are printed on Forms

2210 and 2210F, as well as the free IRS Publication 505, "Tax Withholding and Estimated Tax." If they don't do you any good, try asking someone at your local IRS office, or as a last resort, drown your troubles in a hot bath and a few jiggers of liquid refreshment (not necessarily in that order).

2) Failure to file a timely tax return: five percent per month of the unpaid taxes up to a maximum of five months, or (twenty-five percent). The IRS assessed almost $166 million in delinquency penalties in 1979. During that year about $30 million worth were abated. This penalty will be discussed in detail in Chapter 18.

3) Failure to pay tax: one half percent per month of the unpaid taxes, up to twenty-five percent. This is normally applied to delinquent returns and is in addition to any interest charges on unpaid taxes. When combined with the failure-to-file penalty, the two penalties together cannot exceed five percent per month. After the fifth month, when the failure-to-file penalty has reached its maximum of twenty-five percent, the failure-to-pay penalty can continue mounting up for another forty-five months, or an additional twenty-two and a half percent. It can be applied alone, too, if you filed your return on time but just didn't pay taxes due. It is even applicable to those filing IRS Form 4868, Application for Automatic Extension of Time to File U.S. Individual Tax Return. The two-month extension is granted only to give you more time to fill out your tax return, not to pay the taxes. To avoid the failure-to-pay penalty that would start accruing from the date the taxes were due, you are expected to remit your approximate tax when you file Form 4868.

And how can you do that if you haven't filled out your return, which you reckoned would be so difficult you asked for another two months to do it? As the law is currently worded, you're just going to have to guess (perhaps based on last year's taxes). And what if you overestimate? That's better than underestimating, since the failure-to-pay penalty is applied to taxes owed. If you find you paid more than you actually owed, you can always get a refund, on which no penalty will be assessed.

If an audit has shown you owe additional taxes, the failure-to-pay penalty can start accumulating if you don't pay the additional taxes within the ten-day time limit stipulated by the bill that later arrives. After day ten, it begins heading for its twenty-five percent maximum at the regular rate of one half percent per month. If you contest the additional tax, the failure-to-pay penalty normally ceases to accumulate until the issue is settled. Of course, if you lose the appeal and still do not pay the taxes, the penalty starts accumulating again. According to nationwide averages there is about a nine percent chance of getting it negated on appeal, if you can prove enough reasonable cause as to why it should not be applied, such as that a holdup man got away with all the money you were about to mail to IRS. There were more than 488,000 successful abatements in 1979. But that still left a whopping 4.2 million cases owing $103 million. That's more than the number of tax returns actually examined that year—almost 2.3 million of them, according to the commissioner's 1979 report.

4) Bad Checks: If your check or money order for taxes bounced, the penalty is one percent of the

amount of said check or money order. If it was for less than five hundred dollars, the penalty is five dollars or the amount of the check, whichever is less. This penalty is in addition to any other penalties provided by law; however, it doesn't apply if you "tendered such check in good faith and with reasonable cause to believe that it would be duly paid." One hundred ten thousand bad-check penalties were handed out in 1979, and about twenty-five hundred were abated. The government stands to collect approximately $791,000 in penalties for their efforts.

5) Civil fraud: fifty percent of additional taxes due. This is often assessed when a large, obvious understatement was involved and it appeared to be wilful on the taxpayer's part. If assessed, it negates the failure-to-file and failure-to-pay charges, which could have totaled a maximum of forty-seven and a half percent. However, if civil fraud is not assessed, the five percent negligence penalty can be added to that forty-seven and a half percent, increasing the total to fifty-two and a half percent. 4.6 percent of the 6,818 civil fraud penalties assessed in 1979 were abated. That left over twenty-five million dollars in fraud penalties to be collected. For more about civil fraud, see Chapter 7.

6) Failure to file a timely partnership return. If your partnership return arrives late or incomplete, the IRS may charge a penalty of fifty dollars per partner per month up to a maximum of five months, or fraction thereof.

The following three penalties apply to employers:

7) For every W-2 form on which an employer fails

to include his identification number, the IRS can charge a penalty of five dollars.

8) If the W-2 was not furnished to IRS in compliance with the law, the charge is ten dollars for each form not supplied.

9) Failure to account for and pay over withholding taxes: one hundred percent of taxes due, or twice the amount that would normally have been paid.

There are several other less common penalties, one of which applies to a credit for federal tax on gasoline for nonhighway use. If Farmer Mauve used ten thousand gallons of gasoline on his farm, and claimed twenty thousand gallons for the federal gas-tax credit he's entitled to for nonhighway use, he can be charged two hundred percent on the excess ten thousand gallons. So, if the federal gas tax was four cents a gallon, he would owe not only four hundred dollars in additional taxes, but another eight hundred dollars in penalties! In cases where the excess is very slight, the minimum penalty is ten dollars.

Even though you may not be able to dispute your adjusted tax bill on which penalties are based, you don't necessarily have to take those penalties lying down. Some of them have a good chance of being removed, if you appeal them.

A word of caution, before we go any further: Appealing your penalties does not guarantee their removal, and could wind up costing you more. This actually happened to one unfortunate fellow when he decided to appeal the fifty percent penalty for civil fraud the IRS wanted to charge him for failing to file tax returns. And indeed, they did negate the fraud penalty. But before he had a chance to celebrate, they replaced it with twenty-five percent for failure to file a tax return, over twenty percent for the failure-to-pay penalty, and five percent for negligence. So he ended up paying more than the fifty percent they were originally going to charge. Somehow it took the thrill out of his victory.

Penalties for negligence are among the more common currently imposed by IRS. After all, the logic goes, if the taxpayer failed to pay that much tax, he may have been negligent. Negligence is defined in internal Internal Revenue literature as an "intentional disregard of rules and regulations." The courts went a step further when asked to provide a guideline for applying the negligence penalty: Ask yourself, they told the IRS, what a "reasonable and prudent man" would do, given the same facts and circumstances. With all those negligence penalties being handed out, one may well wonder at tax examiners' definitions of "reasonable" and "prudent." Or maybe it's "circumstances" that's giving them trouble.

Be careful about pleading ignorance when they point out your mistakes. It might work in criminal cases, where they have to prove wilfulness, but civil authorities don't always accept ignorance as an excuse when they assess their penalties. After all, a reasonable and prudent man who didn't know the answers would have asked someone who did know. Aha! And that's just what you did! You were following the advice of your sister, the bookkeeper, who works with taxes all the time. But, unfortunately, her advice turned out to be wrong. Or you tell the auditor, "I know other people who do the same thing," namely deduct furniture as a medical expense.

"That's no excuse," the auditor will say. "They were ill advised, and so are you. Five percent, please." Maybe he'll ask for the names of those "other people," too, while he's at it.

Well, he can't deny this one: "I got that advice straight from the IRS. I did just what the information operator on the other end of the toll-free number told me to do." That may be enough to get that penalty removed. But it can also raise a small problem. Unless you took down the operator's name or recorded the call on your TinEar cassette recorder, how can you prove this statement? On the other hand, how can the IRS disprove it or still claim you were negligent?

You may be taken slightly aback when the auditor refuses to stand by one of the IRS's own. But he knows something you may not: Those information operators don't necessarily have all the right answers. The IRS does try to minimize faulty advice by carefully screening and testing applicants, putting them through six-week training courses, and having them monitored by more experienced IRS personnel from the Examination Division. And sometimes during these eavesdroppings, they do catch erroneous information being passed along. One trainee was telling people they could split a dependency exemption when two family members were supporting a third, which (at the time) was totally incorrect. Well, you can't learn the whole tax code in just six weeks. In fact, no one in the IRS knows the *whole* tax code.

Whether you followed someone else's advice or

your own judgment, the fact remains: Your tax return is deficient, in the auditor's educated opinion. But were you really negligent when you understated your taxable income, or was it just an honest mistake? A new law could have come along that you weren't aware of, or perhaps you had simply forgotten about that extra income the auditor says you owe taxes on. But that doesn't make you negligent, does it? Ignorance is not the most prized of virtues, but it is not negligence. There he goes, though, slapping on that negligence penalty. Well, it's only five percent—averaging $113 per return in 1979—is it enough to work yourself into a lather over?

To some taxpayers it's a matter of principle. They maintain they were not negligent, and shouldn't have to pay for it. To others, it really is a matter of economy: those that owe say, $3,000, are asked to pay another $150 on top of that for something they're not guilty of. You can heat your house for a week with that! So why should the IRS get it?

Not many people bother to contest the negligence penalty. While about 83,000 were assessed in 1979, only 1,492 were successfully abated. That's less than two percent. But for those who wish to retain their squeaky-clean records, the negligence penalty can sometimes be contested, with less inconvenience than you may have thought. You might see it added in right there in the IRS office, after the auditor has concluded his calculations and handed you the results. Right then and there you can make your protest known. If being called negligent offends you, tell the auditor you wish the penalty removed, and tell him why. He probably won't comply with your request, but that doesn't prevent you from going over his head. Ask to repeat your plea to his group manager. If you still can't get satisfaction, your next step is the Appellate Division of the Internal Revenue Service. The auditor or his group manager can give you the address to which you should mail your request for an appeal. But first, ask them whether a written request is necessary under current regulations. If the disputed amount is less than $2,500, they may be able to make the arrangements for you. Under current law, if it's more than $2,500 you must file a formal written protest with the IRS district director.

If you do decide to send a written protest, the Appellate Division will want to know exactly what it is you're protesting. The free IRS Publication 5, "Appeal Rights and Preparation of Protests for Unagreed Cases," outlines other items that must be included in your letter. You could also ask the auditor for the more comprehensive Publication 556, "Examination of Returns, Appeal Rights, and Claims for Refund." You don't even have to wait until you get home to write your letter; you can simply scribble a few lines on IRS stationery before you leave the office, stamp it, and speed it on its way to the Appellate Division. Meanwhile the auditor's report may be sent to his review staff, which could recommend the removal of any penalty. But if they agree with the auditor, be prepared to hear from the Appellate Division, which gives dissatisfied taxpayers a convenient alternative to the courts.

When it comes down to a matter of your word against the auditor's, the IRS appeals officer—known as a conferee—is likely to lean a little toward the auditor's opinion, since the auditor is not only well grounded in tax law, but took copious notes during the audit. Sometimes the auditor's decision to assess penalties is based on your remarks during the audit. And that could form a large chunk of your argument. You may not be able to argue fine points of tax law, but the auditor's subjective opinion of you is something else again. If you plan to dispute it, you ought to have a few notes of your own, taken during or soon after the audit. Request a copy of the auditor's notes, too; he may not hand them over the day of the audit (indeed, knowing you're filing an appeal, he may add to them after you leave). If he refuses to hand them over, you can probably obtain them through the Freedom of Information Act (see Chapter 6). Those same notes will no doubt begin to shape the conferee's opinion, since he will want to be familiar with your case before hearing it. And he'll be more inclined to sympathize with you if you're prepared to answer the IRS's charges with more than just a vague insistence on your righteousness, like "I am not negligent."

Having thoroughly armed yourself for your meeting with the conferee, you need only to discover the time and place—which should arrive by return mail in short order. Somewhere on this document you should find a telephone number, too, which in addition to the conferee's name, will be of paramount interest to you. (If you can't find a number, ask IRS information.) Now you will attempt to save yourself some time and (you hope) money. No matter which penalty you're contesting, or which portion of the tax adjustment, you can start by dialing that phone number.

When the voice on the other end answers, "Appellate Division," ask to speak with the conferee whose name you found on the letter. State your case briefly, giving as many strong, clear-cut reasons as you can for removing that disagreeable penalty. Since all he knows about you is what the auditor told him and the fact that you want to save a hundred dollars or so, he may test your degree of "reasonableness" and "prudence." Again, you're ready to provide ample evidence. You might offer to mail him documentation to support your claims, if necessary: a corroborating letter from an employer or merchant, perhaps, which was not available for the audit. When you notice him starting to sound a little more sympathetic to your point of view, ask him to reconsider the charge. If you can convince him, he may be inclined to fulfill your wishes. It has happened more than once in the past.

After the phone call the conferee will review your return and the auditor's adjustments, and the next thing you know, that penalty could have disappeared. And you didn't even have to go to the trouble of meeting this nice person face to face. (Do you think he'd have found in your favor if he knew you were lounging around in your pajamas when you called him?)

Some appeal cases are too complicated to be handled by phone. If the conferee determines this from what you tell him during your call he may ask you to meet him face to face. If that sounds like too much trouble, you can always give up and drop the case.

Another inexpensive shortcut you might try is to write a letter to the Commissioner of Internal Revenue in Washington. When the matter involves rules and regulations, and the auditor's questionable interpretation of them, briefly outline your objections for the commissioner and ask him for a ruling. It will definitely have an influence on your local IRS officers. Of course, if it's not in your favor, you may not want to call the ruling to their attention.

If you hadn't known about these relatively painless procedures, you could have wasted a lot of time and half a day's work going to the meeting in person; but that's nothing compared to all the waiting you'd have to do if you should take your case to the courts. Whether your case is decided by phone or in person, if you disagree with the Appellate Division's decision, or wish to skip that step altogether, you can appeal to one of four courts. Without paying any taxes or penalties first, you can go to U.S. Tax Court or the Small Claims Tax Court. The latter is a form of binding arbitration which (except in highly unusual circumstances) cannot be appealed by either party, you or the IRS, once the decision is made. It was designed to simplify tax claims of less than a specific amount, currently five thousand dollars, and taxpayers sometimes argue their own cases here without hiring an attorney. An attorney's services can be very helpful, especially where matters of judgment and legalities are involved; but if your case involves tax technicalities, a qualified accountant may be your best adviser.

You're free to seek their assistance at any point during the appeals process.

Choosing one of the three other courts allows you to appeal their decisions to higher courts if they find in the IRS's favor; but since it is a civil matter, the IRS can also appeal. Like Small Claims Tax Court, U.S. Tax Court will hear your case before you pay any taxes or penalties. If you decide to take this step, the IRS requests that you let them know, so they can file a formal letter, called a *statutory notice of deficiency*. This notice will limit you to a 90-day period (150 days if mailed to you outside the U.S.) in which to petition the tax court, after which IRS can start dunning you if you still haven't filed the petition.

If you wish to argue before a jury of your peers, you usually have to pay taxes and penalties first, sue for a refund, wait six months or until your claim is denied, and then your case can be tried in U.S. District Court. That's a lot of trouble if all you're contesting is the negligence penalty. But if you are challenging heavier penalties, like the fifty percent civil fraud penalty, or the amount of additional taxes themselves, going to district court may be worth your while. Just remember, U.S. District Court generally doesn't accept suits against IRS unless you've paid the taxes they claim are due. There have been those who tried to argue against their tax liability, without bothering to pay it first, only to have their cases thrown out of court.

But if you can't afford to pay all taxes due, you might still make it to district court by paying off one portion at a time, and contesting each in turn. For instance, your assessment may be divided into four parts: personal income taxes and withholding taxes for two different years. So, you pay the thousand dollars they claim you owe in withholding taxes for the first year, and sue for a refund of that. If you win that case, use the refund to pay off the next charge, and so on. Of course, if you lose, that may be an indication of how your next suit could turn out, and you might give in to the IRS at that point. It is a gamble: "You pays your money and takes your chances." The fact is, your protest will be brought to the attention of the Appellate Division somewhere along the line, at which point a conferee will contact you to try to negotiate an out-of-court settlement. You don't necessarily have to discuss your case with them, but you might as well pay them a visit at least to find out how much resistance they are putting up. It could save you a lot of trouble. In 1978 almost fifty-five thousand cases were disposed of out of court.

If the tax court rules against you, you can take the case to the U.S. Court of Appeals. You still don't have to pay taxes or penalties to take this step—although interest will continue to accumulate. The same applies if you go on to the highest authority, the Supreme Court. However, they may choose not to accept your case, which leaves the decision of the court of appeals intact.

The higher the court in which your case is decided, the larger region will be affected. For instance, if the final decision was rendered by the U.S. Fourth Circuit Court of Appeals, it will have a greater impact on the IRS in the Fourth Circuit than on others. It's when the Supreme Court hands down a decision that the impact reverberates equally loudly in all IRS districts. At times, though, local IRS offices have found it advantageous to justify their actions based on decisions made in courts outside their own district. In other instances they have chosen not to appeal to the Supreme Court to keep a decision from affecting more people.

There are two courts available to those who pay their taxes and penalties first, in the hopes of recovering them when they win their case. There is the multijudge U.S. Court of Claims, whose decision can be appealed directly to the Supreme Court; and U.S. District Court, the only place where you can have the advantage of a jury. These twelve impartial citizens will be concerned only with the *factual* portions of your case, or: Did you do what the IRS accused you of? Should you be made to pay an additional fifty percent for fraud? Should that thousand dollars you claim was nontaxable income be taxed? If you or your lawyer can present enough evidence proving your innocence, the jury can remove those penalties and/or taxes you're contesting. But it is *not* their place to pass judgment on legalities; that is, the meaning or intent of the applicable laws. Things like "What did Congress have in mind when they passed this law?" and "Can the law be applied to you?" are matters for the judge to decide. It makes sense, since a judge is supposed to know more about legal matters than the average juror.

As with U.S. Tax Court (not to be confused with small claims tax court), you can appeal the decision of the district court to the U.S. Court of Appeals, and then to the United States Supreme Court. (See diagram.)

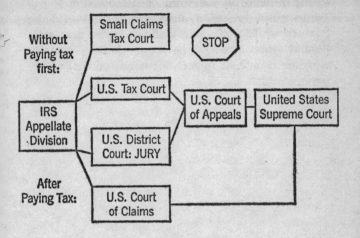

Your chances of having penalties removed from your tax bill, by national averages, range from zero to fifteen percent. Of course, your actual chances depend on your individual circumstances and the penalty involved. Sometimes a simple protest right in the IRS office will do the trick, or an almost-as-simple phone call to a conferee in the IRS's Appellate Division. Taking your case to court is the longer and more involved method of seeking justice, but may be the only way you'll get it. If you have exhausted all the appeals procedures you care to go through and the penalty still stands, try to see it in the spirit in which it was intended: It's there to discourage you from breaking whatever law they used to justify it. So naturally, it is not tax deductible.

The best way to win an appeal is by presenting

strong evidence in your own behalf. Some of it will be in your possession already; but that evidence retained by IRS, like the auditor's notes, may seem beyond your grasp. The next chapter contains suggestions on how to get your hands on that all-important evidence.

CHAPTER 6

FOI:
Getting Into the Act

Once upon a time the government of the United States was about as open as a beggar's palms. It was a relatively easy matter to find out what Uncle Sam was up to; after all, it was designed to be a "government of the people, by the people" et cetera. But then along came war, war machines, military secrets—and an excuse to withhold certain touchy information from the people. They called it "national security," or, what the public doesn't know won't hurt it—and could be to our advantage, to boot.

When it was first introduced, the concept of "national security" really did mean something. The public may have had a right to know what its government was doing, but, they reasoned, enemies had no such right. So they kept such sensitive matters as battle plans and infiltration strategies off the airwaves, and nobody seemed to mind—except the enemy. So, while the war machine fought on under the secure veil of secrecy, the nation at large remained secure as well.

Curiously, the need for secrecy did not end with the signing of peace treaties; at least, not from the government's point of view. It had suddenly become so easy to keep the general public out of government's way, they decided to turn it into a sort of hobby. All they had to do was label a matter National Security or use some other euphemism like Official Use Only, and it was sealed from all but a few lucky eyes. Classified documents began piling up in ever-increasing numbers. Top Secret, Astronomical Secret, Very Sensitive Material, and Don't Even Read This became the order of the day. It got so Uncle Sam's left hand didn't even know what his left thumb was doing. And the public, meanwhile, was left completely in the dark, except the few who got through to a foreign Ambassador. Something had to be done.

Then in 1946 Congress came up with the Administrative Procedure Act, a law designed to give people—all citizens, not just a privileged few—freer access to government documents. This act was supposed to advise both seekers and dispensers of information how to pass it from one to the other. But it was so vague and inexact, no one could be sure whether he was breaking the law or not. So, in 1966, Section 3 was amended, in hopes of clearing up twenty years of confusion. It didn't work. The bureaucrats still couldn't figure out what they were allowed to release and what should remain confidential. Thus, a year later, Congress tried again—more amendments, more hopes, and still more confusion. Finally, in 1974, Public Law 93-502 laid it on the line: The government must either produce the material or tell requesters a qualified reason why they can't have it. Despite the terror that struck certain of the more seasoned legislators at the thought of putting dirty laundry on public display—and despite a presidential veto—what is now known as the Freedom of Information Act (FOIA) is finally fulfilling its long-sought ideal: Doors the U.S. government tried to close to the public can now be unlocked—not all of them, mind you, but quite a few. Behind the others perch our old friends, National Security and its cousins.

With the Freedom of Information Act securely on the books, dozens of revelations began spewing forth exposing the seamier side of our venerated government, no doubt sending our eighth-grade civics teachers into shock. We learned about CIA's ghastly experiments on human guinea pigs, the FBI's vendettas against hand-picked targets, the unorthodox collection and laundering of campaign funds, Watergate's children and stepchildren—oh, it was a gossip-lover's paradise! The press was having a field day, as were nonfiction writers, former government employees, lawyers, researchers of all kinds, and maybe a few foreign spies. Of course, sometimes you had to sift through an awful lot of tripe to get to the juicy stuff. Bureaucratese can make for very dull reading, and woe to the bureaucrat who is not fluent in that particular nonlanguage. So some of their secrets may still be safe.

It's not only the press and other professional writers who have benefited from FOIA. Taxpayers can use it, too, when they wish to see what the IRS has on them besides tax returns. Of course, you shouldn't just walk into your nearest IRS office and say, "Give me everything you have on me, I have a legal right to it." You might get what you ask for if the temperature outside is 102 degrees and it's snowing. No, more than likely, you will be expected to follow certain prescribed procedures. Well, it *is* the government—what did you expect?

Even before FOI required the IRS to comply with taxpayers' requests for information, they were willingly handing out individuals' tax returns to them, plus government tax publications, advice on return preparation, and other unclassified materials—all for the asking. You can still obtain copies of any of your tax returns, from as far back as seven years ago, without bothering to cite the Freedom of Information Act. That step need be taken only if the IRS should balk at your request.

Basically the Freedom of Information Act (also known as "5 U.S.C. 552") was passed so that citizens could have access to information about themselves which is stored in government files. Such information could be especially useful to taxpayers against whom IRS is threatening action—be it civil or criminal. Only under certain conditions, discussed later, will you be allowed access to tax information about other citizens. That's OK with you though, it's *your* file that you are interested in, and the FOIA says you have a right to examine it. However, as is the case with just about every other law, it also designates a few areas "off limits." Things you can legally be denied access to include the following:

1) Classified materials designated as such by executive order (like good old National Security again);

2) Internal information relating to IRS personnel, including rules, regulations, medical and personal records, home addresses and phone numbers, opinions, criteria for determining whether a case merits

further action, and enforcement tactics, such as protecting identities of confidential sources;

3) Trade secrets and privileged commercial or financial information;

4) Inter- or intra-agency memos or letters "which would not routinely be available by law to a party other than an agency in litigation with agency";

5) Certain investigatory records compiled for law-enforcement purposes—both civil and criminal.

These last are what you would be most interested in if you learned the IRS was launching an investigation against you. It is this section that the IRS is likely to cite if they decide to deny your request; but since it is open to interpretation (or misinterpretation), you do have some room to fight back. There are six conditions under which investigatory records can be withheld. IRS will not release information if it:

1) interferes with enforcement proceedings;

2) deprives a person of the right to a fair trial or impartial adjudication;

3) constitutes an unwarranted invasion of privacy;

4) discloses the identity of a confidential source;

5) discloses investigative techniques and procedures;

6) endangers the life or physical safety of law-enforcement personnel.

The record you finally receive may be filled with holes and blacked-out sections that you will not be allowed to examine for one of the above reasons. For instance, you may request an informant's affidavit about you, but all information relating to the informant's identity will be deleted, in accordance with item four. So the statement that originally reads:

I was married to the bum from January 1969 to March 1972. During that time he presented me with a kangaroo coat, a rust Porsche with puce interior, a Transylvanian death mask, and a few other little trinkets—but told me not to ask where he got them from. He's supposed to pay me alimony of four hundred dollars a month, but he's eight months behind and I think he may have skipped town to get out of paying taxes.

... might reach you this way:

I was ... During that time, he ... told me ... he's supposed to ... but I think he may have skipped town to get out of paying taxes.

Very useful. But other records the IRS has in its files may very well be worth the effort of obtaining. Which ones? And what can you do with them, other than start a bonfire? Read on.

If you have been audited and subsequently assessed for additional taxes, and perhaps penalties, you may want to challenge the IRS's figures. In that case it would be a good idea to request the auditor's or revenue agent's workpapers from which calculations were made. You should also ask for any notes he made during the audit, and the forms and schedules he had to fill out listing changes in your deductions and tax liability. Be sure that somewhere in your request (in close proximity to the actual names of the materials desired) you include the word "readable" or "legible" or you're likely to wind up with a mass of undecipherable hieroglyphics.

From these materials you can see what the IRS based your assessment on, and you may spot some errors. If they make the IRS look a little too greedy, you will naturally want to call it to their attention. The auditor may have misinterpreted one of your answers, or recorded it wrong; or maybe you misunderstood his questions, and so left him with the wrong impression. Mathematical errors? Not very likely, but there's always a slim chance. You might run it through your Pik Pocket calculator, just in case.

You should also ask for that section number of the Internal Revenue Code which the revenue agent or auditor is using to justify his changes. There are so many sections and subsections, and amended subsections of sections, there's bound to be some overlapping; and perhaps if another of those numerous sections had been applied, you wouldn't have to pay as much additional tax. One example is the deduction for depreciated property, which is figured differently under Section 1245 than it is under Section 1250. An alert accountant may spot the loophole, come up with a valid reason for applying the other section (whichever is to your advantage), and save you some money.

Remember, whenever you request information from the IRS, always be as specific as possible. The law requires all FOIA requests to be expedited within ten working days of their receipt, except under unusual circumstances when an extension may be granted. But the more information you can provide to begin with, the faster they can process your request. At the very least you should include your name and address, the city in which you believe the records are located, the subject matter, and dates the records were made (such as the day of your appointment with the auditor). No need to request "everything you have on me"; ask only for those records you believe will be useful to you. The disclosure officer can't just push a button and make everything pertaining to you magically appear. He'll be looking only under your name and your district. There may be information connected to you in someone else's file, such as an affidavit you made in a previous year about another taxpayer. Unless you supply that person's name and address or some other identification, they won't even know to look for that affidavit.

If you are under criminal investigation by a special agent, (as described in Chapter 21) you'll want to know what kind of case the government is building against you so you can adequately defend yourself. If you know the special agent's name, include that in your request. Among other things, the special agent will be seeking evidence of wilfulness (intentional lawbreaking) on your part—the item that, more than any other, separates the criminal from the civil offender. He may have a whole folder containing nothing but items of intent—and this information would be most helpful in preparing your defense. You may prevent your case from reaching court if you can clear up some of the faulty items you may find in the "wilfulness" file. For instance, a statement of yours may have conflicted with an accountant's affidavit on you, but you can point out that the accountant wasn't aware of all the facts. When the special agent asked what you took to the accountant, you answered, truthfully, "Everything I needed." But the accountant testified that all you showed him was totals, not actual records. However, he didn't ask for any, even though you were prepared to produce them. So, there goes one item of intent. Now all you have to do is refute the others, and you're home free! Of course, they could refuse this request, citing interference with enforcement proceedings. But you're not trying to interfere; you're just trying to help them learn the whole truth . . . right?

The special agent may also have been remiss in writing his report on you, based on the notes he took during his interview with you. Again, a breakdown in communications could have occurred, giving the agent a false impression, in which deluded state he wrote his report. So you might ask for a legible copy of his notes, as soon after the interview as possible, while it's still fresh in your memory. It is on these notes that he will base his memorandum of the interview—which is something else you should ask for. And if they *are* accurate, they may still give you an idea of the direction he is taking, which may help you to plan your rebuttal accordingly.

Rebuttals, incidentally, are something else special agents consider in preparing their case against you. It is their job to develop suitable answers to your rebuttals—and that's another thing you can request. Pretty soon you could be butting and rebutting one another to kingdom come. Actually the IRS will appreciate your correcting any false or misleading information they were planning to use against you in court; then they can discard that and build on evidence which *is* correct, thereby strengthening their case. But don't let that stop you from calling obvious errors to their attention; your speedy action may just stop them in their tracks.

If you find yourself in the throes of an IRS investigation, any of the above information could be of value to you. However, you may not be granted access to everything you ask for, under the provisions stated previously. You may then accept the decision with quiet dignity, or, as the IRS will inform you, you may appeal it—either to the Commissioner of Internal Revenue, Freedom of Information Appeal, P.O. Box 929 Ben Franklin Station, Washington, D.C. 20044, or to U.S. District Court. The latter is much more costly and time consuming, but may be the only way you can get your hands on those records you're after. On the other hand, the court could agree that the IRS was justified in their denial—so you'll never know what you missed. But if you win the appeal, IRS may have to pay the legal fees. In any appeal case the burden is on them to justify their denial of your request.

In certain out-of-the-ordinary cases a person may ask the IRS for information concerning individuals or entities other than himself. Here another federal law comes into play: the Privacy Act. A third-party request can be denied on the grounds of invasion of privacy and Internal Revenue regulations guaranteeing the confidentiality of tax records. However, you can be granted access to someone else's tax records if the party in question has granted you power of attorney, which should accompany your request.

If a husband and wife file a joint return, either of

them can rightfully request a copy of that return; even if they are divorced when the request is made. However, if one spouse suspects the other of filing a joint return without permission, certain complications can arise. The wife whose husband walked out on her may implicate him for tax fraud by asking the IRS a not-so-innocent question like, "Did my husband file our joint return this year?"

"Do you normally file jointly?" the agent will ask.

"Yes."

"Did you intend to do so this year?"

"Yes, I think so . . ."

"Did you sign a joint tax return this year?"

Oh-oh. The correct answer, no, means she will not get a copy of any such return since the IRS now knows it is not hers. Of course, if her husband had forged her signature on his return in order to claim her as an exemption, they could charge him with fraud . . . another good argument for marital communication.

If she had simply written a letter to her local IRS office requesting a copy of her joint tax return, she probably could have gotten the information without even citing the Freedom of Information Act. The letter would have read, "Please send me a copy of my joint tax return for 19__. My husband's name is _____; his Social Security number is_____." She then would add her own name and social security number and her signature. If she should mail the letter in May, she'll be in for a long wait, since the IRS will still be engaged in posting all the tax returns that came in the previous month. Quicker action can be taken if such a request is received around August or September.

Of course, asking the IRS for a copy of a return you know you didn't file may border on deceit, and you wouldn't think of doing such a thing yourself, would you? But our hypothetical heroine could well find out what she wants to know if the IRS sends her a copy of a joint tax return with her signature forged on it. She could then report her husband for filing a false return, or have him charged with forgery. On the other hand, if the return would have been correct had the signature been her own, it might be to her advantage to ask her husband how much of the refund check he plans to give her, before she reports him to the authorities.

As stated previously, you generally can't just walk into an IRS office and ask for someone else's file, even by citing the Freedom of Information Act. However, there are certain third-party matters that may be disclosed on request under FOIA. They include: information returns of certain tax-exempt organizations and trusts; applications for tax exemption; and accepted offers in compromise. For further information about these, contact the national or a district IRS headquarters.

In general an IRS employee will be extremely careful to establish identification of third parties requesting information on others. He knows very well that he can be sued as an individual for disclosing records to unauthorized people. So he's not going to show your tax return to your ex-wife unless he's positive you gave your permission.

Whatever information you wish to obtain from the

Internal Revenue Service, ask your district office for it directly first. If it is not forthcoming, or you have reason to believe that some of it has been held back, you can always resort to the Freedom of Information Act. A written request, addressed to the disclosure officer of the district in which the records are filed, should read something like this:

> This request is made pursuant to the Freedom of Information Act (5 U.S.C. 552) or regulations thereunder. I hereby request the Internal Revenue Service to make available for my inspection and possible reproduction my federal income tax returns for the years 1978 and 1979 and all documents attached thereto. I agree to pay IRS for the cost of duplication of specified materials, and for search fees assessed on an hourly basis, not to exceed fifty dollars.

Here is why you should write the request this way: *"This request is made pursuant to the Freedom of Information Act (5 U.S.C. 552)."* If you don't cite the FOIA, the IRS may not consider it a formal request, and thus may not comply.

". . . to make available for my inspection and possible reproduction . . ." Many of your records on file at IRS may already be in your possession: receipts, insurance forms, W-2's, and so on. You may want to examine your files first, before deciding what specific items you want copies of, since you must pay the cost of duplication. But if you want the IRS to mail you copies of the whole file, say so in your request.

". . . my tax returns for the years 1978 and 1979 and all documents attached thereto . . ." Describe as best

you can the records you want; the more specific you are, the faster your request can be processed. If you just want to know what kind of file the IRS has on you, ask for all documents pertaining to you for the years you're interested in. You may not want to ask for your tax returns, especially if you already have copies of them. But you might be interested in attachments that were made to those returns since filing, such as an informant's report. Once you've examined the files they have on you, make your selections for reproduction accordingly.

"*. . . I agree to pay IRS for the cost of duplication of specified materials . . .*" If the IRS doesn't find this statement in your request, they'll generally contact you before acting on it, to assure themselves of your willingness to pay. At present the cost of making copies of requested materials is ten cents a page. You may want to call your IRS office to find out their current rates before ordering all four rolls of microfilm and one thousand pages of your tax history to be copied. Of course, if it's only a matter of three or four pages, or if you're deemed indigent (by federal standards, that is), or if you're making this request on behalf of a state or local government, fees may be waived, at IRS discretion.

"*. . . and for search fees assessed on an hourly basis, not to exceed fifty dollars . . .*" Like duplication fees, these are subject to change from time to time. They are presently five dollars an hour for personnel time; and if a computer is used, that will add to your cost. You may or may not want to set a maximum limit on the amount of fees you're willing to pay, but it's usually a good idea. If IRS finds their fees are going to exceed the maximum you specify, they will so inform you, and you may adjust your request accordingly.

Remember to *sign* your request, and include the address where you want the records sent. If your request is for records whose disclosure is limited by law or regulations, such as internal memoranda or business returns, you must establish to the IRS your rights to these records.

Positive identification will be required before the IRS will release information to you. If you hand-deliver your request, take along a photo ID, and you should have no trouble. Two nonphoto ID cards containing your signature may also suffice. Copies of these can be mailed in along with your request, or enclose a notarized statement affirming you are who you claim to be. Again, the IRS wants to be sure that some jerk from Podunk is not trying to impersonate you so he can get hold of records which are none of his business.

Unless you have moved recently and know your tax returns are on file in another district, you should send your request to the Director of your local IRS District Office, Attention: Disclosure Officer. There are seventy-five district headquarters across the country. If you can't find the address in your telephone directory, call the IRS toll-free number, tell them where you live, and ask them to which office you should write.

Sometimes you may find that the answers you seek from IRS can be given over the phone, which can save you a lot of time and trouble. Other times the employee you call may realize you have a problem outside the normal framework of the Freedom of Information Act. The Internal Revenue Service, in a stroke of hindsight typical of responsive government agencies, has instigated a program designed to resolve such problems as billing or payment errors, lost or stolen checks, inability to understand various communications from IRS, and erroneous Social Security numbers. The program may also be helpful during those miscellaneous instances when you think you're getting the runaround. It is called the Problem Resolution Program, for want of a catchier name. Naturally the abbreviation is just as predictable: PRP. Implementing its objectives is its functional stepchild, PRC, for Problem Resolution Committee, consisting of several local department heads in each district, including the district director. During 1978 sixty-six thousand taxpayers were referred to PRP. As the program continues to expand and becomes more visible, referrals are likely to increase, in the hopes of trimming some of the red tape people have encountered just by asking a simple question like "Have you sent me my refund check yet?" If your problem does fit the criteria of PRP, the committee will try to resolve it within five working days. If it's going to take longer, or if they need to refer you to another agency, you should be so informed. And when it's all over, they may send you a letter asking you if you got what you were after, hoping you'll give them passing grades. In this instance at least, the IRS is deeply concerned with projecting what PR men call "a positive image." And you thought they didn't care what people think of them!

* * *

Thanks to the Freedom of Information Act taxpayers no longer need be left in the dark about their IRS files. A simple written request to your local disclosure officer can often produce much of the evidence they have been gathering against you, or their justifications for assessing additional taxes. Keeping in mind the exemptions listed in FOIA, be as specific as possible with your request, so that IRS can process it within the required ten working days. If it is denied, you may appeal the decision to the Commissioner of Internal Revenue for review or to the U.S. District Court. But beware! By the time you've gone through all those bureaucratic channels, you may become so excited by the process, you won't be able to stop. Once having penetrated IRS, you might decide to tackle the CIA next. Happy hunting!

An IRS audit is something you are not likely to forget, especially if you appeal the auditor's findings and make use of the Freedom of Information Act. Even more unforgettable is the very serious experience of facing criminal tax charges. Just how bad a mistake must you make to arouse the suspicion of the Criminal Investigation Division? Why do some cases become criminal ones while others remain in the civil arena? The following chapter explains the differences between the two.

CHAPTER 7

Civil or Criminal?

Bonnie and Clyde are both in trouble with the Internal Revenue Service. But only one of them is a criminal. Bonnie owed $25,000 in back taxes and interest on them, plus an additional fifty percent penalty for fraud. Clyde owed a total of $20,000 in taxes, penalties, and interest on income he should have reported. Bonnie is selling her fur coat and antique-car collection to pay the IRS, while Clyde is busily scraping together the five-thousand-dollar fine he must pay in addition to his back taxes and civil penalties . . . before he begins serving his one-year prison sentence. Bonnie may have been just as guilty as Clyde, but because the IRS felt that her case lacked sufficient jury appeal, she managed to avoid criminal action. In Clyde's case, the evidence—including the testimony of seven reliable witnesses—was so overwhelming, the IRS felt a conviction was practically guaranteed. The U.S. District Court accommodated them.

Being "in trouble with the IRS" does not necessarily make you a criminal. The majority of tax discrepancies are treated as civil matters, and are handled by the Service's Examination or Collection Divisions.

Only when a special agent from the Criminal Investigation Division gets involved might you need to start worrying about fines and jail.

If the IRS is simply assessing additional taxes and penalties, even the fifty percent civil fraud penalty, you might consider yourself a delinquent account, a naughty boy, an absentminded or disorganized bookkeeper if you like—but not a criminal. As long as no special agent is investigating you, your case remains in the civil arena.

The IRS's Criminal Investigation Division works backwards compared to other law-enforcement agencies. While almost everyone else from the FBI to your local police department starts with a crime and seeks its perpetrator, the special agent starts with a suspect and then tries to prove he did something wrong. The factor that determines whether your case will be turned over to the Criminal Investigation Division is not so much *what* you did, but *how* you did it. Nonpayment of taxes may or may not be a crime, depending upon the reasons behind the action.

The one thing a criminal investigator is looking for above all else is *wilfulness*, also known as *intent*. That is, did you deliberately conceal income, or just forget to report it? Did you neglect to file a return on purpose, or because you were confined to a hospital, swathed in bandages, and so full of drugs you lost track of the date? Did your accountant tuck your tax payment into his pocket instead of mailing it in for you, or did you use that money to pay off the mortgage on your boat? If you can satisfactorily prove that your failure to pay the correct tax was unintentional, no criminal charges will be filed.

However, even intentional withholding of taxes may not be enough to arouse a special agent's interest. There is wilfulness, and then there is wilfulness. The difference is in degree. A voluntary, conscious course of action (in the opinion of the IRS agent) could be left to the civil authorities, but if it is also deemed to be stubborn, perverse, without justifiable excuse, with bad purpose—then the criminal aspects are likely to enter in.

The degree of wilfulness is a gray area, something that's left to the better (or worse) judgment of IRS agents during their investigation, and ultimately to a judge and jury if it ever gets that far.

> Congress did not define or limit the methods by which a wiful attempt to defeat or evade might be accomplished and perhaps did not define lest its efforts to do so result in some unexpected limitation. Nor would we by definition constrict the scope of the Congressional provision that it may be accomplished "in any manner."

So stated the Supreme Court in Spies v. U.S. In other words, each case must necessarily be considered on an individual basis. After all, wilfulness is a mental process, and as such, is often difficult to prove. And without proof, there is no criminal case.

Wilfulness is one thing, motive is quite another. You may have had a very good reason for holding back that extra $750 that should have gone to the federal government—like paying for your son's surgery so he could continue to play football. The fact remains, you deliberately withheld your taxes, and you knew you owed them. Technically you could be brought up on criminal charges for this paternalistic manipulation, but your chances are remote. Criminal investigations are generally not undertaken in cases involving less than a thousand dollars of additional tax per year,* or when only one year is involved. However, these criteria don't always apply to target-group projects.

If you happen to be caught by an auditor or revenue agent, you'll probably be required to pay the taxes owed, plus interest and perhaps civil penalties. Penalties may be added at the discretion of the agent assigned to your case, subject to approval by his superiors; or the superiors may just decide to recommend them on their own. If you were caught lying, concealing pertinent records, or your books were inaccurate or altered, they might very well recommend the fraud penalty.

Special agents will be on the lookout for many of these same things; however, their objective is criminal prosecution in Federal District Court. The auditor can only recommend additional taxes and penalties, and the revenue officer is only interested in collecting them. But the special agent is constantly concerned with "jury appeal": Can he get a conviction? He may be dead certain you're guilty, but if he doesn't think a jury will be convinced "beyond a reasonable doubt," he'll leave the matter in the hands either of the Examination or the Collection Division. To recommend the assessment of additional taxes, all the

---

*This minimum amount is subject to change from time to time, depending on current caseloads, sometimes more than $2,000 per year three years in a row.

Examination Division needs is an "indication" of additional income, or unsubstantiated deductions; and the Collection Division is after outstanding taxes that have already been determined.

There are a number of ways for the IRS to uncover tax crimes. The typical case might begin with an audit. In this case the auditor has gone over your bank records, deposits, expenditures, and so forth, and determines that you understated your income by approximately $10,000. Most if not all of it will be subject to taxation, plus interest and perhaps penalties on these additional taxes.

It is during your session with the auditor that the first seeds of criminal suspicion can be sown. Once he confronts you with the error of your ways, you can either frankly admit to your mistake, or staunchly defend your return as accurate. In the latter case you should be prepared to provide all necessary documentation to support your statements, for it is up to you to disprove the auditor's claim.

After paying the government say $2,900 in taxes, you might well resist forking over an additional $3,500 they're trying to get out of you now. So you decide to fight back, and stick by your original return. You produce canceled checks to show legitimate deductions; receipts from charitable organizations; your carefully kept ledger; and your diploma from Digital Doug's School of Accountancy. You even point out a few extra deductions you didn't include on your return because they were so small you didn't want to bother with them. But now you just might go for a refund.

As long as your documentation is legitimate, all well and good. But beware! The Internal Revenue

Service trains its agents to look closely for inconsistencies, inaccuracies, errors in computation, and sources of unreported income. If you added a few digits to that canceled check made out to "Imperial Funeral Home and Day Care Center," the auditor can easily tell by checking the bank imprint in the bottom right-hand corner, which notes the exact amount it debited to your account. Whenever you try to fool or deceive an IRS agent, you risk a civil fraud penalty being added to your tax bill—or worse.

If you really want trouble, give him verbal evidence of wilfulness. "Which set of books do you want to look at?" does not sit well with a tax man. Neither does "I needed that money to invest in stocks (or real estate, or a business deal) ." And if you tell him, "I know the tax law, I knew what I was doing," you just admitted to an item of intent. So later on, if a criminal investigation is launched, this last remark could be used against you. And even if they don't instigate criminal proceedings, that remark could be used to substantiate a civil penalty.

Up to this point no special agent has been involved, and your case is still a civil one. From here one of two courses of action will follow. If the civil route is chosen by the Examination Division, you can expect a letter from the Treasury Department (of which IRS is a bureau), containing the auditor's proposed adjustments, and offering you four choices:

1) If you accept the findings, you sign a consent statement and mail it in within fifteen days, along with your payment. Except for an interest bill that

will subsequently arrive from the Service Center, that will be the end of it.

2) If you don't accept the findings, you have fifteen days to:

    a) Mail in any additional evidence in your defense.

    b) Request a personal meeting with an examiner to discuss your case.

3) Request a hearing with the regional director of appeals.

If you don't answer this letter within thirty days, the IRS will be saddened, but they won't give up. A second letter will eventually arrive, this time by certified mail, advising you how to petition the tax court, if that's your choice. If you still don't answer, don't worry, they haven't forgotten you. A third letter may come your way, more threatening than before; or a revenue officer may darken your door. He will have come personally to collect your taxes, any way he can. And he can be very persistent. It may get rather unpleasant, but at least it's still a civil case.

If you honestly can't bring yourself to agree that you owe the IRS that $3,500, you may want to consider seeking justice before a judge and jury. But you can't very well sue for a refund unless you've paid the tax first. Generally no U.S. District Court will accept a case of a taxpayer contesting the amount of taxes claimed by the IRS if they haven't been paid. This is a matter for the tax courts to handle, or the IRS's own appeals personnel. If they decide against you, you can appeal their decision, but if you want to fight the matter before a jury of your peers, you'll have to risk paying the taxes and hope the district court overturns their decision, at which point you'll get a refund of the money you never believed you owed in the first place; that is, if the IRS doesn't appeal that decision.

In the second course of action, one or more of your previously filed tax returns may have also been examined, and a pattern of consistent underpayment may have emerged. Now your case has been turned over to the Criminal Investigation Division, and the burden of proof reverts to IRS. Whereas before you had to prove their accusations false, the special agent is out to prove them (or some of them) true. And he has more time than his civil counterparts to dig deeply into your affairs. He'll keep on digging until he collects enough evidence to prosecute you, or decides to drop the case because he couldn't find enough jury appeal. The latter happened to a businessman after an auditor discovered a sixty percent error on his returns for two years in a row. Because he had underreported his profits for that period by about fifteen thousand dollars, the case was turned over to a special agent. The businessman explained that he had closed out one of his businesses and transferred its leftover inventory to a new business, and didn't count it as a purchase expense. He claimed he didn't know he had to report it. Since there was no way to disprove his plea of ignorance, the special agent decided against prosecution, and left it to the Examination Division to handle as a civil case. Except for getting out of some penalties, ignorance of tax laws is no defense in civil proceedings.

If the special agent does decide to pursue your case, he will once again lead an expedition through your financial records, this time carefully watching for any statements that don't jibe with your previous remarks to the auditor, or those of witnesses who may have been contacted. He may confront you with evidence of your deceit, such as deposit tickets from a separate bank account that you failed to include on your tax return. If you can't adequately explain them, he has that much more evidence against you. On the other hand, if you can produce incontrovertible proof of your innocence, he may have no choice but to discontinue the criminal investigation.

It's a long, laborious process that could take up to a year (sometimes longer) to complete. The end product will be a detailed report containing your history, the civil aspects of your case (remember, they're still after those taxes and penalties computed by the Examination Division), evidence of income—reported and otherwise—evidence of intent (wilfulness), your proposed defenses and the IRS's rebuttals to them, the special agent's conclusions, and recommended charges such as, "wilful evasion of taxes."

By the time you get to court, the IRS feels that the case against you is fairly solid. Even if you decide to plead guilty or "nolo contendere" the special agent will usually still testify as to your wilfulness. Or, if you think you can show why the charges against you are false, you can plead not guilty. If you are nevertheless convicted, you can appeal, as in all other criminal proceedings, all the way to the Supreme Court, although they have no obligation to accept your case.

Remember, whether you are convicted or acquitted of criminal charges, you are still liable for civil taxes and penalties. The total bill proposed by the Examination Division is likely to be higher than the amount claimed by the criminal investigator, since he will only recommend prosecution based on what he's sure he can prove, beyond that "reasonable doubt."

The Examination Division may claim you owe $20,000, but the special agent thinks he can only prove $6,000 and that is what he recommends prosecution on. However, no matter what happens in court, the Examination Division will still try to collect the full $20,000, unless you can prove you don't owe it. You can contest the difference between what the Examination Division is charging and the findings of the special agent, no matter what you plead.

Some people plead "nolo contendere" so they'll be in a slightly better position to get out of civil penalties, especially the fifty percent fraud penalty. After all, a plea of "nolo contendere" is not an admission of guilt, it just means you're not challenging the criminal charges against you. However, if you pleaded guilty or were convicted, there is little or no chance of successfully contesting those civil penalties, simply because a conviction or a guilty plea constitutes proof of your wilfulness. If you do decide to plead guilty, you might consider paying your taxes before going to trial. This encourages some judges to be more lenient when pronouncing sentence.

One possible way to avoid all this unpleasantness is simply to file an amended return before the IRS contacts you. The amended one says in effect, "I apologize for the errors on my original return and wish to make up for them." The IRS, not one to hold a grudge, will probably accept your apology, along with your back taxes, and that will be the end of it.

Rarely, if ever, will they prosecute after a voluntary disclosure. However, if they contact you first, the IRS will look upon any disclosures you make after that point as admissions of guilt, which they could very well use against you.

What's the worst the IRS could do to you for violating a federal tax law? Make you pay your back taxes plus interest from the date they were due, plus penalties, fine you up to $10,000, and send you to prison for up to five years per each return for which you were found guilty; that is, if three of your returns were found to be fraudulent, you could serve a maximum of fifteen years in prison. Prison sentences and court fines only apply to people convicted of *criminal* charges, and most tax offenses never get that far— especially when they involve only one return, or less than $5,000 additional tax due per year.

When an auditor suspects wilful behavior, he will, as noted earlier, consider turning a case over to the Criminal Investigation Division. When he discovers a large enough discrepancy, this step is practically automatic, only you may not find out about it until a special agent pays you a visit. However, preventing your case from crossing that fine line between civil and criminal infractions is not entirely beyond your control. There are a few precautions you can take during an audit, even if you now realize you made a little mistake when you prepared your return:

1) Answer the auditor's questions carefully without volunteering excess information. The IRS trains auditors to establish rapport with taxpayers, in which

relaxed atmosphere you might be tempted to reveal more than you had intended.

2) Don't be too quick to parade your knowledge of tax matters before the alert tax examiner. After all, how can we be expected to keep up with the tons of confusing and ever-changing tax laws Congress keeps passing? The more you appear to know the more intent they could charge against you later.

3) Keep your personal expenditures estimates on the conservative side—within reason, of course. You'll learn why in Section II.

4) Carefully check the auditor's findings, remembering that you can have your accountant review them for you later. But for now, if you think the auditor's figures are reasonable, and especially if you know you did something wrong, go ahead and remit your payment. Compared to a criminal investigation, it only hurts for a minute.

PART II

How the IRS Proves Income

For 1979 the Commissioner of Internal Revenue reported gross internal revenue collections of over $460 billion. During the same year the IRS gave back about $41 billion in refunds. Also during this time they spent around $770 million on their examination and appeals program to assess $5.4 billion in additional taxes; to which they tacked on an extra $1.8 billion in penalties for good measure.

If you do a lot of tedious digging, you could learn the methods the IRS uses to prove the existence and taxability of unreported income. This book will save you from all that trouble, by conveniently compiling eight different methods of proof all in one place. In the following chapters you will find simplified descriptions of seven indirect methods: Net Worth, Bank Deposits, Source and Application, Expenditures, Unit and Volume, Cash "T," and Percentages; plus the direct method known as Specific Items, as employed by both civil and criminal investigators.

By learning how each of these methods uncovers taxable income, you will have the kind of advantage few adversaries enjoy: an inside track—the better to anticipate their next set of moves and plan your own, in a game where the rules were once known chiefly to the opponent.

Just as you can make mistakes on your tax return, so, too, can the IRS falter when proving your income later on. Some of these miscalculations can cost you additional taxes, even though you reported all income and can verify your deductions; so it could be to your advantage if you know how to look for them. In the final chapter of this section you will be made privy to some of the more common flaws inherent in each of the eight methods.

Keep in mind that both direct and indirect methods are used primarily to verify tax returns or to show additional taxable income, if any. Direct methods may show refunds due; however, indirect methods seldom show grounds for tax refunds. In the latter the findings are circumstantial, but they often do successfully support the IRS in court cases. In civil cases it is usually up to the taxpayer to prove he doesn't owe additional taxes. However, in criminal cases the burden of proof is on the government, so they will take greater pains to charge you with only what they can readily prove.

We recommend you read the following chapters in order, lest the final chapter escape your grasp. We begin with the civil version of Specific Items, a kind of introductory lesson in IRS methodology which might or might not lead them to an examination of your gross income.

CHAPTER 8

The Most Direct Way to Your Money

SPECIFIC ITEM I: CIVIL

The only thing some people ever get from the Internal Revenue Service is tax forms, which they obediently fill out and return by April 15. The rest of the year the IRS is about the furthest thing from these fortunate citizens' minds—and vice versa. But one day the IRS decides they'd like to get to know you better. Somewhere along the line you get a sneaking suspicion they were not altogether satisfied with one of your tax returns. It hit you like a flash—the moment you noticed, among the junk mail, your Skateboarders' Newsletter, and bills, a certain official-looking envelope from the Internal Revenue Service.

Maybe they're just writing to thank you for your timely payment, you think doubtfully, or to confirm your address . . . but of course, no such luck. As soon as you unfold that letter, your suspicions are confirmed. The IRS wants you, and not for a charity ball. They're interested in specific deductions and are using the most direct method for questioning them.

Like a dating service, it lists the name of the auditor who has been selected just for you, plus his office address and phone number, and the time and date you are expected to appear at his desk, which you may change if it's inconvenient. There the similarity ends. For what matchmaker would tell you to bring financial records with you—especially on the first date?

The form letter from IRS contains a long list of specific items related to your financial affairs, including bank records, business transactions, and deductible expenditures. You are relieved to discover that they do not want you to bring records of *all* of them to the audit, only the few with a check mark beside them. Your relief may grow when you discover they did not check off one or two of your "maybe" deductions which had been giving you cause for concern. However, that's no guarantee they won't be questioned during the audit. Once you show up with those check-marked items (provided you can dig them all up), there are any number of directions your examination could go. But from the indications on that letter it appears they simply want to verify a few deductions via a direct method called Specific Items. At least that's where they'll begin.

Your invitation to the audit could request documentation for items on last year's return, or a previous one filed up to three years ago. Of course, you'll be delighted when you unearth every record the letter asked for, which will prove beyond a doubt that you were entitled to those deductions. But what if you can't find one of those checked-off items? Will you lose the deduction just because you don't have written proof of it?

Not necessarily. A lot depends upon how good you are at debating. If you're the timid, withdrawn type, chances are the auditor will walk all over you. However, if you were bold enough to take that deduction or credit in the first place, you should call upon that same courage to defend it. An audit is no place for contrition.

Suppose the letter told you to bring all your bank statements from two years ago. After pillaging every drawer, closet, crate, cranny, and shelf in your house and office, you can only turn up half of them. They were in the first place you looked, the file folder where you keep all your bank records. You simply cannot understand where the other six statements could have disappeared to; no matter how hard you rack your brain, you still can't imagine where else to look for them. Now what?

Well, you could gather together whatever canceled checks and deposit slips you can find corresponding to the missing months; or you could ask your bank to pull the statements out of their files and copy them for you—for which they'll probably charge you a search fee. Then there is another alternative, which may prove the easiest of all: You can call the auditor at the number printed on your letter, and tell him candidly that you couldn't find some of those records he asked you to bring. Ask for his advice. If he wants to see those bank statements badly enough, he might even activate that IRS machinery designed to extract information from banks. So the auditor finds your records for you, saves you the time and expense of getting them from your bank yourself—all because you made one simple phone call.

The preaudit phone call has other advantages as well. In the case of deductions for which you never had any written proof—such as a charity donation—you might ask the auditor what would convince him of your honesty besides a receipt. He might suggest you obtain a signed letter from the recipient of your generosity, affirming you really did give that worthy cause the approximate amount you claimed; or perhaps he'll think of some other form of documentation which hadn't occurred to you. Again, this could save you (and the auditor) some time and prepare you better for the audit.

If Virgil Butterfinger had only made such a call, his case might have been wrapped up months earlier. Virgil had legitimately claimed a year's worth of laundry bills as a business expense on his tax return. His employer required him to wear a clean uniform to work every day, although the employer would not pay for the cleaning. Virgil explained all this to the auditor, but the auditor wanted more proof than just Virgil's word. However, that was all Virgil had, since he'd neglected to save any of his laundry receipts. Even the receipts would not necessarily have proved he had all that cleaning done for business purposes. Now the IRS expects Virgil to pay taxes on the money he spent to have his uniforms cleaned. But Virgil knows he was entitled to that deduction. He's getting his employer to write the IRS a note to that effect, and his dry cleaner to affirm that Virgil was a steady customer. If the appeals officer accepts this evidence, Virgil will have won—the hard way. Had he known to bring those testimonials to his audit—something he could have learned by phone—the additional taxes might never have been assessed.

If you took the standard deduction, you may be surprised to learn that the IRS still wants to check some specific items. As you might see from the check marks, their interest could lie in certain tax credits or business expenses you claimed in addition to the standard deduction. For instance, if you claimed mileage and various other expenses connected with the car you use for work, the auditor may want to see some proof—not only receipts for the expenses themselves, but evidence that you really used that car for business and not personal driving. You may have claimed only seventy-five percent of your auto expenses as a business deduction because you figured you used it for nonbusiness purposes the rest of the time; the auditor will want to know how you arrived at this division. So tell him—but do it with *conviction*.

The main goal of a Specific Items audit is to find out quickly and directly if you did something wrong on your tax return. Rather than reconstruct your entire fiscal year, they choose to spot-check a couple of items with a high probability of error, such as might have been caught by the DIF program described in Chapter 4. If you bring in all the receipts they demanded of you, it should be a relatively painless matter to match them to your return and thereby verify its accuracy. But perhaps they happened to ask for one receipt you've lost or misplaced. You've brought the auditor everything else he asked for: every check you wrote all year, business ledgers, and proof that you pay more than fifty percent of your mother's support, which qualifies her as a deduction. It all makes you look like the honest, upstanding citizen you are—except for one missing receipt from a now-defunct insulation dealer, with which you claimed the energy credit.

You remember this fellow insisted on being paid in cash for the insulation, so you have no canceled check to prove you bought it. After the guy delivered it, he scribbled a receipt on the flap of a used envelope, which you promptly filed away, with the intention of claiming that tax credit. Now that audit time has arrived, though, the makeshift receipt is nowhere to be found, and the auditor is threatening to transform that credit into a tax bill. You offer to show him your attic with its two-year-old layer of insulation.

The auditor doesn't bite. "That doesn't prove you bought it that year, nor does it tell me how much you paid for it," he says.

"Well, what *would* it take to prove it?" you ask. "And don't say 'the receipt' again. I've already told you I lost it."

"That's what they all say," he answers wearily.

"But I am telling the truth! Look here," you intone, pointing grandly to all the other records you lugged down to the IRS office. "Didn't I bring every other receipt you asked for? That should show you I'm not the kind of person who cheats on taxes."

"Yes, and I'm allowing all these other deductions for which you showed me receipts. But I can't allow this energy credit. Sorry," he says, drawing a line through it right before your eyes.

"Hold on a minute!" you shoot back. "The law does not say you *have* to disallow something, just because I can't prove it. Are you really disallowing that just because you don't believe me? Would it help if I swore to it on your IRS manual?"

The auditor looks sympathetically upon your downcast face, trying not to let your protestations sway him. "It's not up to me to prove you can't have the credit," he explains; "you're the one who has to prove you *can* have it."

"I see," you say. "Well, suppose I write to the IRS commissioner about this?"

"Was he there when you installed that insulation?"

"Of course not, but . . ." Suddenly you see a way out. "That's it! My wife was there; so was my mother, and my kid! And Wild Willis from down the block came over that day, too, and he compared the price of his insulation with mine! They'll all back me up!" you cry. Now you're getting somewhere.

"Now we're getting somewhere," says the auditor. "Maybe you can have that credit after all."

Never be shy about asking questions in defense of your deductions. If you're sure you had a right to it, state every reason you can think of. And if the auditor still won't allow it, ask which regulation he's using to justify it. He may point out that the burden of proof is on you, but if you create enough doubt in his mind over what is and what is not allowed, you may send him scurrying for his copy of IRS Publication 17 or 334. Most auditors have one or both of these booklets right on their desks—or in close proximity to them.

If you can get him to quote a relevant passage, that may give you more ammunition. Now you can argue about definitions of key words in the regulation, or different ways of interpreting it. Maybe you claimed one third of your phone, electricity, and heating bills and half a bedroom as a home-office expense. Now you can dazzle him with your interpretation of the regulation that allowed you to take that deduction; define words like "room," "regularly," and "customers" as you believe they were meant. After a convincing enough performance, the auditor may very well restudy his Tax Guide. Before you take to the "stage," however, be sure the facts really do support your arguments. As Chapter 7 pointed out, an overt display of tax knowledge could help seal the doom of the guilty.

On the other hand, your brilliant performance could go for naught. All your strong arguments, expert opinions, and demonstrated knowledge still have not moved the auditor to your side. But what's this? Is he trying to add a negligence penalty on top of the extra tax? Now that's hitting below the belt.

You may not even find out about an added penalty until a bill from the IRS arrives in your mailbox later on. Phone the same auditor and ask him why it was put there.

"I didn't put it there, the review staff did," he might say.

So ask for their phone number, and put the same question to one of them. And don't take "It's our policy when that much tax is due" for an answer. That penalty implies you were negligent, when in fact it was simply a matter of your misinterpreting a tax law or misplacing a receipt. That certainly doesn't make you negligent, especially when you did try to find out whether or not you could take that deduction before you claimed it. If you still can't get satisfaction, you might want to appeal to the Appellate Division.

One of the most common items of contention is business deductions for travel and entertainment, especially when it's a matter of your word against the auditor's. You know you did a certain amount of traveling and entertaining on behalf of your employer, but having kept no written records (except perhaps an incomplete datebook), you settled for an estimate when you filled out your return:

"Hmmm, seven thousand miles—no, more like eight thousand. Nah, make it eighty-five hundred . . . At least twenty nights in motels," (at that point your mind drifted to fond memories of that wonderful night at the Hoboken Holiday Hostel . . . then, back to the tax return): "Oh, yes, twenty-five nights in motels, that makes, mmm, seventy-five meals at about ten dollars, maybe fifteen dollars apiece—oh, yes, and that night we went all out to entertain Mr. Hogstuffer at the most elegant night club in town: Let's call it three hundred dollars. Let's see, that comes to approximately—make it a nice round figure—five thousand dollars. Close enough!"

"Oh, yeah?" says the auditor almost two years later. "Got any proof?"

You fumble around for your old datebook, and flip to the pages you entered appointments with out-of-town clients, when you thought about it. That ought to satisfy him, you think. But it doesn't.

"What do you want, a whole notebook with every little trip I took, complete with mileage?" you ask, half in jest.

"That's about what I had in mind," the auditor

shoots back, much to your surprise. "And if you had also included some indication of the purpose of each trip, and who you contacted, I'd know whether it was really a legitimate deduction or not."

"Well, you can start with these guys," you say, pointing to the names scattered across your datebook. "They'll tell you I was there on business, all right."

But the auditor probably won't bother to call those people. Even if he did, there's no guarantee they could remember a meeting they had with you some two years ago, when dozens of people might visit them every day. So don't be surprised if he cuts that travel and entertainment deduction down to the bare minimum.

"Six dollars a day for meals!" you cry; "I spend more than that on breakfast!" Next time you'll know to keep records of those expensive meals. (Sometimes they won't allow anything for meals without at least a record kept in current manner).

Another source an auditor might employ is a report your state revenue service supplied him. If your state income-tax return was audited and found slightly deficient, you might have gone ahead and paid the paltry amount of additional taxes they assessed, without thinking much of it. But U.S. tax-bracket percentages are usually higher than states', so the federal tax on that same understatement could be five times as much as your state charged. Now, that's a figure worth fighting. Explain to the auditor that the state assessment was so low, it wasn't worth your while to contest it. Set the record straight: If you believe your original returns were correct as filed, stand by them, even though your acquiescence to the state looks like an admission of guilt. The IRS is not necessarily bound by state tax auditors' findings.

A special note to those who have incorporated a business: If a discrepancy turns up on your personal or corporate return (whichever is being audited), the tax man may need to find its source. Sometimes it turns out to be a "business expense" claimed by the corporation, but not allowed. For instance, if your corporation paid a decorator $10,000 to have your personal residence remodeled, it should not have been counted as a deduction on the corporation's return. Likewise, you should have included it as dividend income on your individual return (more on this later). If the IRS discovers that $10,000 was omitted from both returns, they are likely to tax both entities for it. The corporation will be assessed at the corporate rate on the full amount, and you will be asked to pay personal taxes, also on the full $10,000. It matters not who was audited first, you or your corporation; once the discrepancy is found on one return, the IRS may go on to any other returns that are affected. In any case the auditor will attempt to find out if deductions are legitimate or if income is being concealed, even if it means examining both ends of the same deal. After all, that's his job.

As your audit progresses, the tax examiner may run across evidence of undeclared income or unsubstantiated deductions. Even if these are not related to the specific items he originally asked you to verify, he may still decide to alter his course of action and delve a bit deeper into your finances. He might even do a gross-income test on you (described in the following

131

chapters), to see if you reported what you should have on your return.

What are some of the things that can tip off a tax man? For one thing, there are your bank deposits. He might add them all up to see how close the total comes to your reported income. If they total very much more than what's listed on your return, he'll want some explanations. Now is the time to point out which of those deposits were nontaxable, like redeposits, checks to cash, or transfers of funds. If you can't whittle those deposits down to within a reasonable distance of your reported income, he may begin to wonder about you.

Going through your canceled checks, he might notice there were none for food or clothing. Could it be you used another bank account for those expenses, which you didn't want IRS to know about? He can get a fair idea of the way you live by noting to whom your checks were paid: a gardener, your exclusive exercise club, an exotic travel bureau. Does your lifestyle match the income you reported? Or are you living beyond those means?

Now he may begin asking you about expenditures not even listed on your return for which you did not bring any documentation—because he didn't ask for it in that letter. Not many people can remember how much they paid for personal living expenses two years ago. If the auditor starts asking you about such things, don't just toss him the first likely figure that pops into your head. If it's wrong, he could get a distorted picture of your income, which could lead him down a faulty path. Instead, beg his patience until you can go home and check your records. If he's going to do a gross-income test—which takes into account *all* income and expenditures, deductible or not—you want to be sure he starts with accurate information. However, you need not assume a Specific Items audit will turn out this way. If the letter tells you to bring only your medical expense records and proof of your moving expenses, that's all you need to take. Nothing more.

When you get a form letter from the IRS Examination Division asking you to bring several checkmarked items in to an audit, it's a good bet that the auditor will be employing the Specific Items method to verify or challenge certain questionable deductions. If you don't bring in everything the letter requests, the auditor may disallow some of those deductions, unless you can find some other way to prove them. Asking for his suggestions, even by phone before the audit, can sometimes do the trick. How well you come out could depend on your skill at argumentation.

Some Specific Items audits can turn into gross-income tests if the auditor stumbles upon evidence of an understatement while asking routine questions. Remember, just because the auditor found a few deficiencies on your return does not necessarily mean you'll be sent to jail. Other than assessing taxes, interest, and penalties, the worst the Examination Division can do to you is refer your case to the Criminal Investigation Division—and *they* are the ones who can get you sent to prison. But none of these is likely to take place until they get a fairly accurate picture of your gross income, which is then adjusted to determine tax liability. Very often it is done via an indirect method of proof, seven of which will be detailed in the following chapters.

CHAPTER 9

How Much Is That Net Worth?

Before the IRS can determine how much you owe in taxes for any year, they have to know how much you made, and of that, how much is taxable. Now, if all taxpayers were scrupulously honest bookkeepers, it would be a simple matter just to compare their books to their tax returns to verify those carefully tallied figures. However, when people began under-reporting their income on their books as well as their tax returns in order to avoid paying higher taxes, the IRS began to realize they would have to dig a little deeper to uncover the true figures. Thus were born indirect methods of proving income which the taxpayer failed to report directly. This chapter will deal with one of these methods, Net Worth.

You may not have any nets, but, if you're like most shoppers, you do have a net worth. It is the difference between what you own and what you owe at any point in time. What the IRS looks for are changes in net worth, that is, the difference between what you were worth at the beginning of the year and what you were worth at the end of the year. To figure your net worth change (see illustration 1), you subtract all your liabilities from all of your assets at both points in time—the beginning and end of the year. Then subtract the beginning-of-the-year figure from the end-of-the-year figure, and you get—that's right—your increase or decrease in net worth. If it's a positive figure, especially if it's a large one, the IRS will be very interested to know what brought about the increase. And if perchance the result of all this tabulation turns out to be a negative figure—better luck next year.

Illustration 1

1/1/78	12/31/78
Assets	Assets
— Liabilities	— Liabilities
Net Worth 1	Net Worth 2
	— Net Worth 1
	Net Worth Increase

Once the IRS determines the difference between your beginning net worth and ending net worth, they don't stop there. Next they'll add in all your nondeductible expenditures during the year—food, clothing, the toy guillotine you bought for your kid, the vet's bill for your dog's surgery, the grass shampooer for the garden, and anything else you purchased which has not been listed as an asset. They'll also add in the federal taxes you've already paid, and things like nondeductible life-insurance premiums. At this point they'll even add in any expenditures you made that normally qualify as itemized deductions. When they subtract from this total such nontaxable items as inheritances, gifts, nontaxable portions of capital gains, and anything else they don't feel like taxing (which isn't much), they finally arrive at your adjusted gross income, known in the trade as AGI. (See illustration 2).

Illustration 2

Net Worth Increase (from illustration 1, remember?)
+ Nondeductible Expenditures
+ Expenditures Qualifying for Itemized Deductions
− Nontaxable Funds
―――――――――――――――――――――――――――
Adjusted Gross Income

You may think this is the figure they're going to base your taxes on, but there's more. (Hang on, it's almost over!) You'll be happy to know it's a subtraction this time, something you'd already thought of when you filled out your tax returns. Yes, exemptions and allowable itemized deductions, or the standard deduction. You may wonder why they would subtract something they'd just added in. It's because all figures used to compute your itemized deductions may not be deductible themselves. For instance, you may have paid two thousand dollars in medical expenses, but you were only allowed to deduct six hundred of it. However, they had to include the entire amount you spent in order to arrive at your adjusted gross income.

Are you still with us? Illustration 3 may help.

Illustration 3

Adjusted Gross Income (from illustration 2)
— Exemptions and Deductions
―――――――――――――――――――
Corrected Taxable Income

Now all they have to do is compute the tax on the corrected taxable income and subtract the taxes you already reported and paid, and there you have it: the additional taxes owed. And while they're doing all this figuring, they may throw in a few penalties for good measure (civil fraud, failure to pay on time— take their pick) and interest for late payment. Now, think of all the trouble you could have saved them if you had just reported your income correctly in the first place! And many times they do net worths for several years in a row, which runs down the batteries in their calculators even more.

Of course, before they can even begin doing all this math, they have to have a set of facts and figures to plug in: all your assests and liabilities, all of your expenditures, and all those other adjustments we've just waded through. And where are they going to find them? Are you going to tell all? Maybe, but they have their doubts. After all, you've already left a lot off of your tax return (they strongly suspect), so why would you suddenly turn honest now, just because they accuse you? So they begin looking elsewhere.

Just as the IRS has devised indirect methods of proving income, so too have they come up with methods of uncovering information for use with those indirect methods. After getting all they can out of you, they'll visit your bank and make a thorough study of all your records there. Then they'll go on to such fascinating reading as county real-estate records, brokerage records, county lien index, federal and state income-tax returns, and other records. And as they learn more and more about your financial affairs, they collect ever more leads to additional sources you may be concealing. The point is, even if you don't tell them about all your assets and liabilities, they'll probably find out about them anyway, on their own.

Even if they don't find everything they suspect, chances are they will have uncovered more than what appears on your tax return. The IRS is becoming increasingly adept at locating other people's money—and they were good at it to begin with. Wouldn't you love to have someone like that working for *you*?

Once they've compiled this long, humiliating list of your assets, plus the liabilities you willingly supplied so you wouldn't look too rich, their values must be established. You bought a $7,000 car in February? That goes in the "assets" column. But hold it! You still owe Millie's Boutique and Finance Company $6,142 on that car. Don't worry, that gets put in the "liability" side. You might point out that your car is no longer worth the original $7,000; if you sold it tomorrow, you'd only get $5,999 for it, tops. Unfortunately for you, however, personal assets are not depreciable for tax purposes. As long as you own that car, an IRS Net Worth computation will insist it's still worth the full $7,000. On the other hand, you can depreciate business property right and left. Or at least right, and maybe left . . . sometimes. (If this sounds confusing, try reading about it in the Tax Code!) Ask your accountant. If he's not sure, ask the IRS. Even they may not be sure; remember, they are not bound by what they tell you.

The IRS may choose the Net Worth method because of the poor state of a taxpayer's books. Maybe you don't bother keeping any books at all, or if you do, they're so deplorable you can't bring yourself to let anyone else see them, especially someone who knows as much about bookkeeping as an IRS agent. If you do present them for his perusal and his reaction resembles that of an all-star watching a bush-league game (or a stifled variation thereof), he might be thinking to himself, "Guess I'll have to do a Net Worth on this one." And if your books *are* in good, accurate shape, they may still choose the Net Worth method if they find other evidence that contradicts them, or simply because that method appears the most workable.

Besides all your visible assets, bank accounts, and property, they have to add in whatever cash you happened to have on hand, both at the beginning and at the end of the year in question. This can be the most difficult item to prove. If the figure for it is wrong, it can throw off the whole tabulation and leave the IRS with a false basis for calculating your taxes. If you tell the tax man that you had $25,000 lying around the house for a rainy day, for instance, and the next year you were left with only twenty bucks (it rained a lot that year, you recall), that will obviously make a significant dent in your net-worth increase, or decrease, as the case may be.

Of course, if you do tell the agent you had that much cash on hand, he's not likely just to take your word for it. He'll want to know where the cash was kept, who else knew about it, whether anyone ever counted it, the denominations of the bills, when it was spent, and on what, and whether any records are available with respect to the stashed cash. If you could show it to him, let him count it himself, that ought to satisfy his curiosity—but that's only the twenty dollars you claim to have had left at the end of the year. Can you prove you really had that $25,000 you say was on hand, at the beginning of the year? On the other hand, can the IRS prove you did not have it? That could be enough to get the case dropped. But if it's not—especially if it's a criminal investigation—it's up to the IRS to disprove your statement. One crafty fellow told a special agent he kept two hundred thousand dollars worth of twenty-dollar bills in a safe deposit box. The IRS proved by demonstration a box of that particular size could not hold that many bills.

Another big area of dispute can be the "personal living expenses" category. Remember, that's one of those adjustments they make after they determine your net-worth increase, to arrive at your adjusted gross income. Remember, too, that these expenses go in the *plus* column, thus increasing the eventual total on which they will figure your taxes. So the higher you estimate living expenses, the higher the additional tax will be. Now, if the agent has come to your home with his portable Net Worth kit, he can get a pretty good idea of your spending habits just by glancing around him. If you reside in a twenty-seven room mansion containing no fewer than ninety-nine light bulbs, assorted appliances, electric barbecue grills, and lawn sculptures, don't tell him your average power bill is only $9.50 a month—unless you can verify it, of course. Keep your estimates on the conservative side, yes, but within reasonable limits. If you happened to have saved all of your receipts for personal purchases during the year, wonderful! But very few people do, it seems, at least very few taxpayers under IRS investigation. Be as accurate as you can in your estimate, and, if you can't provide exact figures, at least don't *over*estimate your personal living expenses. A mere ten percent overestimation of your grocery bill could cost you an additional hundred dollars in taxes. For example, the Humperdincks, a married couple earning $23,000 in taxable income a year, which makes their tax bracket about thirty percent, paid $3,000 for food one year. But they estimated they had spent $3,300. The extra $300 will show up as additional living expenses beyond what the Humperdincks actually paid. Accordingly the IRS will assume they made an extra $300 and charge them an additional $90 in federal tax. Later their state will assess another $20 or so when the federal government sends its findings to the state tax authorities (Most states have this reciprocal agreement with Washington; is yours one?) Remember, an increase in *liabilities* will reduce your bottom-line figure, so don't forget any of them, not even that $100 you borrowed from your brother-in-law.

Your business dealings, as mentioned earlier, will be figured into your net worth, too. Under this particular indirect method, the IRS is not going to be very interested in your gross receipts or cost of goods sold. As the name implies, they will be looking for *net* changes in your assets and liabilities between January and December. You could have taken in $4 million that year, but if you spent $3,900,000 for deductible business expenses, and used the rest to pay off a loan, your net worth increase for all of this will be $100,000; decreasing your liabilities increases your net worth. In pursuit of that bottom line, the IRS will try to ignore income and paid business expenses and concentrate instead on "Net Worth 2 minus Net Worth 1." Remember, expenses and profits are not used to compute net worth.

In the process they will be interested in your inventory statement. Was it accurate? Can you prove you paid $50,000 for that particle board for your building-supply business? Are you sure that was the sellers' cost to you and not your marked-up selling price? It can get rather involved, since often more than one person was keeping track of inventories, and omissions, misplacements, communications problems, and other mistakes could throw it off. To establish accurate inventory figures the IRS agent will attempt to corroborate the inventory figures shown on your tax returns with your own admissions, statements of your employees who took inventory, or copies of inventory records.

Other items of dispute include failure to adjust your totals for nontaxable income (gifts, inheritances, and so on); the holding of funds or other assets as another person's nominee; the carrying forward of net operating loss from a previous year; a claim that some friend or relative loaned you money; and assets held jointly by you and your spouse. These and other shortcomings of indirect methods will be discussed in detail in Chapter 15.

In common with all indirect methods, Net Worth does not actually prove how much taxable income you took in during a given year, except circumstantially. However, a lot can be inferred from a net-worth statement: If you had a large net increase from the beginning of the year to the end, where did the money come from? If your liabilities were reduced drastically, how did you manage it? It can be assumed the difference is an approximation of your income. For example, say you began the year with a net worth of $50,000 and ended with $60,000. You spent $8,000 on personal living expenses during that time, and had no likely source of nontaxable income, such as inheritance. From this it may be concluded that your adjusted gross income must have been at least $18,000, although you reported only $10,000. In civil cases you will be assessed accordingly and required to pay the additional tax, unless you can prove the income was nontaxable or falsely computed. Sometimes the taxpayer does have a valid explanation: He may have sold assets, like an artwork, not on the original list, or perhaps he was repaid for a loan.

Although there is no statutory authority for the use of the Net Worth method as evidence, case law has established it as admissible for criminal tax cases. A leading precedent was set in 1954 in *Holland* v. *U.S.*, when the Supreme Court outlined broad principles governing the use of net worth in court. The high court held:

> If the increase in net worth substantially exceeds reported taxable income, an inference is justified that

the defendant has received income that he failed to report.

The same decision requires the IRS, if possible, to check out leads supplied by the taxpayer under investigation, which, if true, might establish the taxpayer's innocence. This also applies if the information came to light after the investigation was completed but before the beginning of a trial. Chances are the investigator may already be checking into the matter you brought to his attention, such as loans or cash hoards; but if what you tell him is so flimsy as to preclude the possibility of a follow-up, the agent may simply decide to let it go. In the end the court will be the one to decide.

Remember, a net-worth statement in and of itself will not be enough to prove to a court that you wilfully understated your income. For criminal purposes the IRS must also offer a likely source from which it sprang, such as your salary, medical practice or business, or at least negate all nontaxable sources of income, and then offer proof of your wilfulness. If your loot was ill gotten—through embezzlement, graft, kickbacks, or the like—then the IRS may have to prove about the same thing as the public prosecutor would. The law they will be citing against you will be different from the one the police would choose, but your punishment, if convicted, could be similar: imprisonment, fines, court costs, or a combination thereof.

Net Worth is just one of several indirect methods employed by IRS for proving income. It may be the method of choice when the taxpayer's books and records are unavailable or inadequate. Because it only shows the adjusted difference between what you were worth at the beginning of the year and what you were worth at the end, it may not be a completely accurate indicator of your income. However, it is enough to go on, as far as civil authorities are concerned and they can compute your additional taxes based on a net-worth statement alone. Criminal investigators must establish a likely source of the income indicated by your net-worth increase in order to file charges. Some of the more common items that may throw the totals off are cash on hand, personal living expenses, unreported liabilities or assets, nontaxable income such as gifts, and improperly reported inventory. These should be checked carefully for accuracy. It may be the one time when you don't want to boast about your wealth . . . unless it's nontaxable.

CHAPTER 10

Money in the Bank

Wherever dollars flow, the Internal Revenue Service knows about it—at least, they would like to know. In pursuit of taxable income, IRS agents will go just about anywhere they think monetary transactions have taken place, just to make sure Uncle Sam is getting his cut. And since so many of these transactions occur in banks, it's not surprising that practically every bank in America has had visits from IRS agents. They are about as free to examine your bank records as you are. If your banker refuses access, they simply hand him a summons, legally requiring him to open those files. Since they know they can be fined up to $1,000 and sentenced up to one year in prison for refusing, most bankers will comply.

It's not as if anything were out of order, after all. But it's irregularities, or clues to them, that the tax men will be looking for. Pity the poor, bored agent who must sift through pages of perfectly ordinary, orderly bank records, day after day. No wonder he gets so excited when something irregular turns up! It's like a breath of fresh air, after all those maddeningly common balance sheets.

But you don't particularly want to excite an IRS

agent—not that way, at least. In fact, you'd rather he got bored out of his skull going over your records. That could very well happen, if all your records are exactly as you said they would be. But it's because he wasn't satisfied with your answers to his questions that he has decided to poke a little deeper into your affairs via an indirect method of proof. In this case he has chosen the Bank Deposits method to compute your income, reported and otherwise.

If you have deposited fairly even amounts of money into your bank account at fairly regular intervals—or even intermittent ones—where did that money come from? The IRS assumes it to be your income.

As the name implies, the Bank Deposits method is used to determine your income by matching all the money you've spent during the year with the amounts you deposited into your bank account over the same period. The total debits (checks, drafts, etc.) to your account are subtracted from your total expenditures to arrive at the amount of additional funds you had available outside of your bank account, which are then figured into your income. The formula is as follows:

> Total Deposits
> + Currency Disbursements (outside bank)
> + Noncash Income
> _____
> Total Income Items
> − Redeposits
> − Nontaxable Income

Gross Receipts
— Cost of Goods Sold
— Business Expenses

Net Profit
+ Capital Gains Adjustment

Adjusted Gross Income
— Deductions and Exemptions
— Taxable Income Reported

Additional Taxable Income

Let's take it step by step.

Starting with your reconciled bank balance as of January first, they add in your *total deposits* for that year, as recorded on your deposit tickets or bank statements. From this they subtract your end-of-the-year bank balance to arrive at the amount of money that was drawn from your bank account. When it is less than your total expenditures for the year, which they will or have already determined, they assume the difference was paid in cash. These *currency disbursements* are added to your bank deposits, along with such noncash income as forgiveness of debts or transfer of property in lieu of payment, or a barter agreement, such as performing a service for someone in exchange for an object of equal value. This total—deposits plus currency disbursements plus noncash income—is tantamount to your income for the year, which must now undergo some adjustments for tax purposes.

Not all of your deposits or funds used for expenditures (you will hasten to point out) will be taxable.

The IRS will obligingly isolate these *nontaxable items* from the rest of your deposits, and subtract them from the subtotal they've accumulated so far, in order to figure your gross receipts. Nonincome items may include U.S. Savings Bonds you have redeemed during the year, loans repaid to you, loans received by you, sale of assets such as your house or car, gifts, inheritances, transfers of funds from one account to another, redeposits, bank errors, return on capital, federal tax refunds, insurance proceeds, income from previous periods, decreases in cash on hand from the beginning of the year to the end of the year, and checks made out to cash—which could have been redeposited. Those checks to cash may have been spent, too, in which case the money is probably already figured into currency expenditures; but if IRS can't prove what happened to those checks to cash, they may have to pass up the opportunity to tax it. The more nontaxable items you produce, the lower your overall taxable income will be, and hence the lower your tax liability. So this is a category you'll want to concentrate on, when it comes to decreasing your taxable income.

Further deductions will lower that total even more. If you have a business you now subtract cost of goods sold and all other allowable *business expenses*, including allowable depreciation, from your gross receipts figure. The *cost of goods sold* expense is figured by adding the amount of purchases to the inventory you had in stock at the beginning of the year, then subtracting whatever inventory was left over at the end of the year, thus:

```
  Inventory 1-1
+ Purchases
  ─────────────────────────
  Goods Available for Sale
− Inventory 12-31
  ─────────────────────────
  Cost of Goods Sold
```

After deducting cost of goods sold (COGS, as they sometimes abbreviate it) and business expenses, you wind up with your net profits. To this they add the taxable amounts of *Long-Term Capital Gains,* such as a percentage of your profit from the sale of a house. (They would have first subtracted your entire proceeds from such a sale as nontaxable income.) From then on everything else is subtraction: *exemptions and deductions* which you've probably already claimed on your tax return (if IRS is still allowing them) and the taxable income you have previously *reported.* You may wish there were a few more subtractions, because the final total may show you had more taxable income than you originally reported. The higher your *additional taxable income* is, of course, the more additional tax you'll have to pay. And now that the IRS knows about it, you could be in for more trouble than you bargained for. If wilfulness was involved, you may not only have to pay the taxes and interest, but a fifty percent civil fraud penalty plus—if you're convicted in court—fines and court costs; and you might have to serve a prison sentence. Not every taxpayer whose income is analyzed via Bank Deposits is the object of a criminal investigation, but this method is used more by criminal investigators than by their civil counterparts.

NOTE TO THOSE ON AN ACCRUAL BASIS: If you consider transactions complete at the point of sale, beware of "double trouble," that is, being credited twice for the same expense. Whenever an accrual taxpayer is being examined, corresponding adjustments must be made. A decrease in accounts receivable from the beginning of the year to the end of the year indicates you received funds that were reported as income in a prior year, and therefore should be subtracted from the calculation as nontaxable income. Increases in accounts payable from the beginning to the end of the year should likewise be subtracted, since they represent deductible business expenses not actually paid. Conversely, increases in accounts receivable show additional income not yet received nor available to spend; this amount should be added to the Bank Deposits calculation. However, decreases in accounts payable should not be added in separately since these outlays should already be accounted for under "Currency Disbursements," in the form of money paid out for expenses you had deducted in prior years. So, adding it in again would erroneously inflate the bottom-line figure by that amount.

There are a number of reasons for using the Bank Deposits method, not the least of which is that its admissibility in court has been established by case law. In 1930 the Court of Appeals overturned a lower court decision favoring one taxpayer Gleckman, who had claimed that the government could not prove that his deposit slips reflected specific taxable income. Its decision set a precedent that has stood numerous other court tests since:

. . . if it be shown that a man has a business or calling of a lucrative nature and is constantly, day by day and month by month, receiving moneys and depositing them to his account and checking against them for his own uses, there is most potent testimony that he has income, and if the amount exceeds exemptions and deductions, that the income is taxable. . . . The bank deposits and large items of receipts by Mr. Gleckman do not, therefore, stand entirely alone as the sole proof of the evidence of a tax due from him, but they are identified with business carried on by him and so, are sufficiently shown to be of a taxable nature.

An IRS investigator might choose the Bank Deposits method if no books or records are available, or if the taxpayer refuses to show them to the IRS; or if the records are inadequate or incomplete and don't reflect true income. However, the accuracy of a taxpayer's books—or the lack of it—need have no bearing on the selection of the Bank Deposits method for proving income. In fact, IRS doesn't have to justify using it at all. They may just decide it would be the easiest to manage, under the circumstances.

One interesting—and infuriating—aspect of the Bank Deposits method is that, once all the figures have been entered, it is very hard to alter the bottom-line total. For almost every "minus" sign, there will be a "plus" sign to cancel it out. Thus, if you are presented with an unreported taxable income figure that makes your follicles turn somersaults, you may begin racking your brain for something that will reduce that incredibly high total. (Oh, if only your friends could see this sum, or your campus rival, or your teasing cousin from Southeast Hampton—anybody but the IRS!)

"I just remembered!" you scream as if infused with heavenly inspiration. "I spent another twenty thousand dollars on my business that you didn't include there."

"What exactly was it for?" the tax man wants to know.

"Uh, er, ummm—bugs!" you cry, noticing a large cockroach making its way up the agent's leg.

"Bugs?" he asks, cocking his head skeptically. "You mean, insects?" he inquires, slapping absently at his knee.

"That's it! We had—termites. I had to spend twenty thousand dollars on exterminators!"

"I see," answers the tax man, grinding the roach into your expensive Oriental carpet with his muddy shoe. This expenditure is not reflected in your checks, so he inquires, "Do you have a receipt for the work?"

Triumphantly you produce a small document smelling of Malathion from Boopsy's Bugout for $20,031.45. You smile smugly to yourself as you watch the agent coolly adjust the "Business Expenses" portion of your schedule. You're already mentally counting the extra tax money you're saving, but then—he seems to be taking longer with that computation than he should be. What's he doing, anyway? Well, he is doing what any other tax man would be doing when you try to throw an additional deduction into a bank-deposits calculation. He's not only subtracting from business expenses, but adding that $20,000 to your list of currency disbursements, which increases your total income, as well as your gross receipts, by the same amount as the deduction (see formula). And so, dear taxpayer, you end up with the same tax bill as before. The $20,000 that came off under business expenses went right back on under currency disbursements. Well—easy come, easy go. . . .

One instance when it's possible to decrease the bottom line can pop up on those few occasions when total debits to your account exceed total expenditures, leaving a negative figure to enter in the "Currency Disbursements" slot in the formula. Since that doesn't conform to the IRS's expectations, they simply discount the possibility that you could have spent less than what was debited to your account, and enter a big fat 0. Maybe there were some redeposits you forgot about, or all your expenditures couldn't be traced. Don't try to convince the tax man he made a mistake; zero currency disbursements is the lowest he'll go. But what if you come up with another business expense after the calculations have been made? In that case only that portion, if any, above the difference between debits and expenditures will be added to the "Currency Disbursements" section; then the expense will be subtracted from gross receipts, to reduce your bottom-line total. For instance, say all debits to your account totaled $50,000. But they could only find $48,000 worth of expenditures made during the tax period. Instead of entering "-$2,000" under "Currency Disbursements," they enter "0," and proceed with the calculation. The sight of the bottom-line figure startles you into remembering another two-thousand-dollar business expense for which you paid cash. Since $2,000 was the actual amount by which your debits exceeded expenditures, the "Currency Disbursements" figure remains zero, but the two thousand dollars is deducted under "Business Expenses," and your bottom-line total suddenly looks a bit more appealing—two thousand dollars more appealing, to be exact. This sort of thing does not happen very often, mainly because when tax examiners suspect you'll have a lot of untraceable debits, they probably won't choose the Bank Deposits method in the first place.

You may also be able to decrease that bottom-line taxable income figure by adding in more nontaxable income items that you may have forgotten about, or proving you did not really spend all the money listed under currency disbursements; that $1,000 you contributed to Goodwill, for instance, could have been in old clothes instead of hard cash. Point that out to the auditor immediately.

Of course, even if you didn't spend it, that doesn't necessarily mean you didn't receive it. Instead you could have held onto it, which would just increase your cash on hand. And in the Bank Deposits method, an increase in cash on hand is treated as an "expenditure." And the expenditures that exceed debits to your bank accounts, don't forget, comprise the circumstantial evidence that indicates you had income in excess of your deposits. That's what indirect methods are all about: They provide circumstantial proof that you had income in the approximate amount listed. The Bank Deposits method, for example, says in effect that the money which flowed through your bank account can be considered income. For criminal purposes the IRS must also prove that the income was current, and must identify a likely source for it such as a business, or at least negate all nontaxable sources.

It's not only your bank accounts—checking and savings—that are examined when this method is being employed. Brokerage house accounts, investment trusts, and any other deposit accounts are fair game, too. If you have more than one bank account in different banks, different cities, or under fictitious names or special titles, these, too, can be uncovered through various investigative means. An informant may tip off the IRS, for example, or a clue may pop up on another record under examination. Treasury currency reports, which banks must file with the U.S. Treasury whenever they handle transactions for individuals of $10,000 or more, may also point the way. In any event they will make every effort to uncover *all* of your accounts, hidden or out in the open.

Unlike the Net Worth method, the Bank Deposits method requires no firm starting point from which to build. Where Net Worth is concerned with the difference between what you had at the beginning and at end of the year, Bank Deposits represent what happened during the year. However, as with Net Worth, cash on hand again comes into play; it could account for some of those deposits, as could the sale of personal assets. If the cash on hand had been accumulated prior to the tax period under investigation, it obviously would not be counted as current income subject to taxation. Likewise, the sale of personal assets, and the subsequent deposit of receipts from such sale, would have to be adjusted in accordance with return of capital or capital-gains deductions. Only a certain percentage of your profits on long-term capital gains is taxable, not the entire sale price. Another court decision, *Kirsch* v. *U.S.*, established guidelines for nonincome items in criminal cases involving Bank Deposits, when it said:

> It is one thing for the [the government's witness] to say, in effect, ... that he had exercised all of the means he reasonably could to determine how much of a bank account was income, had eliminated all that he could determine was not income, and was therefore assuming for the purpose of calculating taxes due that the remainder was income, and quite another and different thing to say in effect . . . My evidence shows that all of these deposits were not income, but I do not know how much was not, I have made no effort to find out. So I am . . . casting the burden on the defendant to show, if he can, how much is not. . . . The latter procedure cannot be approved.

In other words, it is up to the criminal investigator to prove beyond a reasonable doubt which portion of those bank deposits was income, or eliminate all nontaxable funds. The burden of proof is not as heavy for revenue agents, who will simply calculate the taxes they believe to be due, leaving the taxpayer to disprove any false or incorrect calculations. If you think you can, feel free to challenge the revenue agent; but be careful that you don't inadvertently increase your taxable-income total (unless you want to pay more taxes). That can be easy to do, even while you're racking your brain trying to decrease it.

The money a taxpayer deposits to banks and brokerage accounts, together with his expenditures, constitutes circumstantial evidence of income. After nonincome items, such as loans and redeposits, have been deducted, as well as business expenses, deductions, and exemptions, the result is taxable income. Once determined, this bottom-line figure may be difficult to alter, since additional expenses, for instance, may be subtracted from one category but added to another, and the one category will cancel out the other one. Thus, Bank Deposits reports showing additional taxes can be like IRS agents: No matter how you try to get rid of them, they just won't go away.

CHAPTER 11

Follow That Income!

Prudence Paleface had never been so embarrassed in her life. It took three days for her usually mousy, sallow cheeks to fade from the ruby flush that had overtaken them. But the thought of all those personal questions—from a total stranger yet!—could bring on the look of the postworkout jogger all over again. Why, even Prudence's own mother wouldn't have the gall to pose such probing questions! But then, the IRS thinks nothing of going where mothers fear to tread. Honestly, that government agency has no shame whatsoever. . . .

Actually Prudence should have been ecstatic. She got off rather easily, compared to many other taxpayers who are subjected to the IRS's microscope. The auditor, who had proved her income through the Source and Application method, considered her one of his most disappointing and tiresome cases. She didn't even have any deficiencies—monetary, that is. After going through all her expenses, purchases, sales, loans, accounts, ledgers, and canceled checks, he could not come up with one shred of evidence of unreported income, which IRS would have been delighted to tax. What a waste of time!

It's a good thing he didn't transmit his disappointment to Prudence. She felt she had been exposed, stripped naked. Money is a private matter, she has always maintained, not fit for open discussion, especially not in mixed company. Prudence kept all her financial matters to herself, as was proper, never dreaming the government knew, or wanted to know, so much about them. Now that they know everything she spent money on last year—*everything,* for heaven's sake!—what would become of her? Now that they know how much she makes, they'll never leave her alone! Nothing but outstretched palms would greet her the rest of her life. She might as well plaster her life savings all over the billboard beside the interstate.

Back at the IRS office the auditor went on to examine the four other taxpayers on his schedule for that day. By the time he'd reported for work the next morning, he had forgotten all about Prudence Paleface.

When a taxpayer gets called into a local IRS office for an audit, the auditor's objective is to ascertain as quickly as he can any discrepancies connected with the tax return(s), and, if he finds any, in what amounts. For reasons of speed and convenience, since they have so many other cases to process each week, auditors are fond of using the Source and Application method of proving gross income. As long as the taxpayer supplies accurate information, the auditor can expeditiously arrive at the bottom line simply by filling in the little spaces of a neatly printed Source and Application form (Number 309), which the IRS supplies in abundance. On the top half is a list of your applications of funds—what you spent or applied money on—while the bottom half contains all your sources of funds—where the money came from. The bottom-half total is subtracted from the top, leaving the taxpayer's understatement of income (if any), which is then subject to taxation. The assumption is that if the taxpayer spent the money, it must have been income—unless he can prove otherwise. If it is an insignificant amount—less than one percent of your total income, say—no additional taxes are likely to be assessed. After all, the Source and Application method is not that precise. Of course, if the total sources (bottom half) turn out to exceed the applications above, the remainder will be a negative figure, which may still be an indication of unreported income. It could mean you're not disclosing all of your applications to the auditor, and he may then wonder what else you are hiding from him.

In order to fill in those spaces on the form, the auditor is going to need your assistance, of course. That's where all those "personal" questions come in.

"How much did you spend on groceries last year? . . . Well, estimate from the receipts you did keep . . . Do you belong to any clubs or organizations? . . . Because I need to know if you paid any dues . . . Mmmm-hmmmm . . . Now, did any of your relatives or friends die last year, and leave you any money? Aw, now, don't cry, I'm just trying to do my job. . . ."

Of course, you want the ultimate total to reflect what is on your tax return, lest Uncle Sam think you a cheater. Unless you have a photographic memory that can pinpoint every financial transaction you had during the year within one tenth of a cent, you'll be sure to take along a healthy set of books, records, receipts, canceled checks, invoices, deeds, and so forth. Then, when the auditor asks you, "How much did you spend for electricity last year?" you can produce your canceled checks to Power to the People of Peoria, which tell a pretty reliable story. The auditor may even add them up for you, since he happens to be engaged in so much addition anyway.

(Quite naturally you didn't bring these records to your audit unless they were requested. But if these questions are suddenly being asked by the auditor, it may be best to say, "Let me get my records.")

That power bill is just one of a long list of personal and family expenses, which he will list on a whole different form. From this he will derive a single figure for the "Personal Living Expenses" portion of the "Applications" half—space number eight, to be exact. (See sample form at the end of this chapter.) Among other items the IRS thought to include in the "Personal Expenses" category are: laundry, education, entertainment, household expenses like mortgage payments and insurance, deductions you may have itemized on your tax return, medical bills, real estate taxes, and alimony. It is here that some Source and Application computations can start to go off track.

Since an excess of applications over reported sources can be taken by IRS to represent unreported income, you want to make sure the auditor does not add in more than was actually spent. He may know very well that before entering the full amount of your

auto insurance under "Applications," he should subtract the hospitalization portion if you deducted it on
your tax return. If he has already counted all medical
expenses from your return, that hospitalization could
be listed twice, thereby erroneously increasing your
total applications. Unless you keep an eye on him, he
may inadvertently double you up into a higher tax
bracket where you don't belong. So if you catch him
adding your entire "education" bills from Uncle Alfie's University for the Unexceptional, part of which
you (legitimately) deducted as a business expense,
wave the red flag like crazy. Point out to him that a
portion of tuition and transportation to Uncle Alfie's
is already being counted as a "Business Expense", and
you don't wish to be debited twice for the same expenditure (part of which was nontaxable in the first
place.)

Keep an eye peeled, too, for interest charges the auditor may unintentionally slip into the "Repaid
Loans" category (space number six). When he comes
to the "Loans" section, be sure he consults the ledgers
that state the amount of principal you paid, instead
of adding together your canceled checks to the lender,
which include both principal and interest. Remember, the interest portion of those checks will already
be counted as a business or personal expense. So if
the auditor now adds the face amounts of those
checks as an application, that interest will be counted
twice.

To avoid "double trouble," keep all of your deductible items in mind while the auditor is entering
those applications. It might be a good idea to make a
list of them before heading for the audit, so none are

overlooked during the rush. Among the items you should pay close attention to are interest on your credit-card payments, and taxes added to your mortgage payments. Anything you deducted on your federal tax return should be accounted for only once on the Source and Application form, or else your "Application" total will wind up unduly high. It may be difficult to remember to separate the deductibles from the nondeductibles, especially when they've been added together on some of your bills, but if you miss some, the two halves may not balance.

Of course, a thorough auditor will be sure to elicit from you *all* of the expenditures he can, even those not listed on the forms. Once he has filled in all the preprinted categories, he will politely ask you what other expenditures you made during the year. Maybe you collect antique baby buggies and bought a dozen more last year. And don't forget that used dentist's chair you purchased to watch your soap operas in. And then there are the major purchases. If you've been making long-term payments on things like cars or boats, the Source and Application form has a separate category just for them. It also includes things like jewelry, furniture, stocks, bonds, appliances, and loans to others. If you're not sure which category some of your purchases fit under, the auditor should be able to help you out. Or maybe you'll put your heads together and come up with a brand-new category. There are extra spaces in the "Applications" section for just such contingencies. These may include options to buy certain property, and start-up costs for a new business.

Other "Application" items they did include are: increase in bank accounts—which should be arrived at only after your balances have been reconciled; increase in inventory, which can be obtained from your tax return (assuming it's correct); loans repaid during the year—excluding interest, don't forget; increase in accounts receivable; payments on business equipment; real-estate purchases; and taxes paid. (The sample form on page 142 shows how these are arranged.)

How are you going to remember all those expenditures? Well, if you pay for a lot of things by check, the canceled checks should definitely jog your memory. You can also refer to any receipts you happened to save. But for cash purchases for which you have no receipts or other records, you're just going to have to estimate as closely as possible. If you've had a lot of cash transactions, you could get to be very good at it; you may even get yourself a guest shot on some TV guessing game.

A word of caution on estimating: keep it conservative—within reason, of course. If you weigh 380 pounds, the auditor will be very skeptical if you tell him you spent only two hundred dollars on food last year. On the other hand, as noted earlier, a mere ten percent *over*estimation of your grocery bills could cost you an additional one hundred dollars in taxes. Remember the Humperdincks from Chapter 9? They were the married couple earning $23,000 in taxable income a year, putting them in about a thirty percent tax bracket. Though they only spent $3,000 on food the year they were audited, they estimated their grocery bills to be $3,300. That extra $300 shows up on the bottom line when sources are subtracted from applications, and the auditor computes it as unreported income, for which the Humperdincks are assessed an additional ninety dollars in federal tax. Perhaps later on they get a bill for twenty dollars or so from their state tax agency, with whom IRS will probably share their findings.

Contributions, which you most likely deducted on your tax return, also have a corresponding space on the "Personal Expenses" form. But if they happened to be noncash contributions, like the five hundred dollars' worth of old clothes you gave to Goodwill, be sure to point this out to the auditor, or he'll just transfer the amount you listed on your return into your "Applications" section, again throwing the total off. In fact, any noncash expenditure—like trading your tractor for five hundred pounds of cattle feed—should be brought to the auditor's attention, or he'll assume it's a cash application.

Once the auditor has listed where all your money went last year, he goes on to the equally fascinating story of where it came from. He'll start with your income-tax return, which he happens to have handy, where (if you have them) he will find your business profits and depreciation deductions. The latter are not really income, in the strict sense of the word; but loosely defined, depreciation refers to an allowable expense for which no money was paid that year. Therefore it was still available to spend. And in this one instance the IRS will be a little loose.

If you don't know anything about accounting, you may wonder at the curious way the auditor is figuring your business sources. Instead of subtracting purchases and expenses from gross sales, he's adding together your *net* profit and depreciation. But don't worry, he has already allowed for your increase in inventory—in space number two, under "Applications," so the end result will be the same. Let's plug in some figures and see.

Computation 1 shows how you normally arrive at net profit.

Computation 1

(A) Beginning Inventory	_____	$ 3,000
(B) Purchases	_____	+30,000
Available Inventory	_____	33,000
(C) Ending Inventory	_____	−4,000
(D) Cost of Goods Sold	_____	$29,000
(E) Gross Sales	_____	$50,000
(D) Cost of Goods Sold	_____	−29,000
Gross Profit	_____	21,000
(F) Other Expenses Actually Paid	_____	−11,000
(G) Depreciation	_____	−2,000
(H) Net Profit	_____	$ 8,000

Computation 2 shows how the auditor will use your figures to determine the funds you had available for other expenditures, while computation 3 shows the same result using actual monies that came into your business, and monies actually paid out by it.

Computation 2

(H) Net Profit	_____	$ 8,000
(G) Depreciation	_____	+2,000
	Inventory Increase _____	—1,000
	(C) — (A)	———
	left to spend:	$9,000

Computation 3

(E) Gross Sales	_____	$50,000
(B) Purchases	_____	—30,000
(F) Other Expenses Actually Paid	_____	—11,000
	left to spend:	$9,000

So, either way you figure it, you wind up with $9,000 left to spend.

The third space under "Sources" has been known to cause a few headaches, because it's so easy to get wrong. This is where you must remember what you took in from any assets you might have sold during the year. And not just your net profit, but the gross selling price, even though only part of this total may be taxable. You see, at this point they're not as interested in segregating taxable income from nontaxable as in establishing where you got the money you said you spent, listed under "Applications." So if you bought that used dentist's chair with the $200 you made on the sale of one of your baby buggies, make sure you reveal this sale to the auditor, or the $200 that is listed under "Applications" could wind up as unreported income, which the auditor is eagerly waiting to tax. True, you may be taxed on the profits from the sale of that baby buggy, at the current capital-gains rate. But wouldn't you rather pay taxes on the $80 above what you originally paid for the buggy than on the full two hundred you sold it for? One reluctant taxpayer who failed to grasp this principle steadfastly refused to report the income he had received from some of his assets, including a tractor he had traded at a profit. When the special agent assigned to his case finally discovered these sales, the figures in the "Sources" section of the form suddenly aligned themselves with those in the "Applications" section and the criminal case was dropped. He still had to pay some additional taxes, but not as much as was originally computed.

Other items in the "Sources" section are gross salaries, nontaxable gifts, inheritances, decreases in bank accounts (checking, savings, etc.) and increases in loans, since some of the money you spent could have been borrowed. After filling in these preprinted spaces, the auditor will ask you what other sources of income you had during the year which IRS left blank spaces for. You may be a bit reluctant to tell him about your bingo winnings, or that extra money you earned for painting over the graffitti that keeps popping up on your neighbors' walls. But those amounts may turn up as unreported income anyway, if you've already revealed all your applications. Remember, the auditor is ultimately out to find the difference between sources and applications, so omitting some of your resources after you've reported all your applications could increase that difference by those amounts.

It is taxpayers' reluctance to reveal additional sources that sometimes causes undue harm. They fear they will be taxed on all those additional funds, so they're inclined to withhold the whole truth. But when it comes to nontaxable sources, have no fear. Revealing them to the auditor will not thrust you into a higher tax bracket; it will merely explain where some of your "Applications" money came from. You should be perfectly willing, for instance, to let him know about any decreases in cash on hand you had from the beginning to the end of the year (unless it leaves a discrepancy on the previous year's return—but let's stick with this year for now). Undeposited money you spent during the year could go far toward explaining some of those applications, and keeping your grand total in line as well. So could your federal tax refund for prior years, which a lot of taxpayers forget is a nontaxable source of funds. Also, remember that only part of the profits you made from sale of assets—personal or business—will be taxable; if you sold them at a loss, you should still report the full sale price. It won't be taxed, but it will help to balance the two halves of the Source and Application form. And that, lest ye forget, is your ultimate goal. Remember, by refraining from reporting all sources of funds, you could leave some of your applications unaccounted for, which will show up as unreported income on the bottom line.

Once the auditor has finished filling in the Source and Application form, and after you've collected your books and records and gone on your way, he may want to check some of your figures against those of appropriate third parties—banks, creditors, customers, anyone you dealt with during the year. He may write them a letter, asking for verification of certain figures you supplied which may not be quite accurate. From there it's a simple matter to compute any additional taxes you may owe.

If your applications of funds exceed your sources—that is, if you apparently spent more than you took in—the IRS will assume the difference to be unreported taxable income, unless you can prove otherwise. This will be added to the taxable income you did report on your tax return to establish your new tax liability. For instance, if you reported $10,000 of taxable income on your return, pushing a single taxpayer to about a twenty-four percent bracket, and your understatement was $20,000, your corrected taxable income is now $30,000. That pushes you up to approximately a forty-four percent bracket. Your total taxes will be figured up to this higher rate, taxes you already paid will be subtracted, and you'll receive a bill for the difference with interest and perhaps penalties added. And the only evidence they needed for civil purposes was that Source and Application form the auditor filled out.

If the two totals turned out equal, or close to it, wonderful! They will probably assume your tax return was correct as filed, and you won't owe any additional tax. However, if during the audit you revealed some new sources of taxable income, you will receive a bill covering them in short order. If the newly revealed sources were nontaxable, so much the better. No more taxes to pay.

If sources exceed applications, your "unreported income" will be a negative figure indicating some of the things you applied money toward were not listed (an investment you forgot, perhaps, or an overlooked donation), or else you underestimated some of your expenditures. It does *not* mean you will get a refund. Like other indirect methods, Source and Application schedules are used for two major purposes: 1) to verify quickly the accuracy of tax returns, or 2) to disclose unreported income for tax purposes.

Other IRS agents besides tax auditors use the Source and Application method. Revenue agents make regular use of it. Special agents sometimes use it as reference material when cases are turned over to their Criminal Investigation Division from Collection of Examination. This could happen, for instance, when a large understatement turns up on the same taxpayer two years in a row or more. The special agent will then probably make a thorough inventory of the figures to verify the Source and Application report. Or he might do one himself to corroborate the findings he arrived at through some other method.

The following page contains a sample Source and Application form. You might like to fill it out just for fun, to see how well you did on your tax return, or to find out what it feels like to be an IRS auditor, or just to kill an hour or so until *Celebrity Ping Pong* comes on.

SOURCE AND APPLICATION OF FUNDS

	ITEM	AMOUNT
APPLICATION OF FUNDS	1. Increase in bank accounts *(checking, saving, etc.)*	$
	2. Increase in inventory	
	3. Increase in accounts receivable	
	4. Payments on business equipment purchased	
	5. Payments on real estate purchased	
	6. Loans repaid during year	
	7. Payments on personal assets required *(auto, furniture, etc.)*	
	8. Personal living expenses *(list on Form 4822)*	
	9. Taxes paid *(all not deducted on business schedule)*	
	10. OTHER:	
	11.	
	12.	
	13. Total funds applied during year ⟶	
SOURCE OF FUNDS	14. Business profit reported per return	
	15. Depreciation deduction per return	
	16. Sale of assets *(gross)*	
	17. Increase in loans	
	18. Decreases in bank accounts *(saving, checking, etc.)*	
	19. Salaries *(gross)* Husband_____ Wife_____	
	20. Gifts or inheritances received	
	21. RECEIPTS FROM OTHER SOURCES:	
	22.	
	23.	
	24. Total funds reported available during year ⟶	
	25. Understatement of income *(Line 13 minus Line 24)*	

CHAPTER 12

Where There's a Till,
There's a Way

Hortense Bedfiller thought she had it made. From strutting the streets in slinky body suits, she had risen to the summit of her profession to become owner and operator of the most sought-after brothel on the outskirts of town. No more whiskey-breathing men forever climbing in and out of Hortense's bed; now she had a whole stableful of high-priced beauties to do the work, while Hortense raked in all that money, skimming off her seventy-five percent and redistributing the rest to her faithful "employees." Never having been one to fool with tax returns, she saw no reason to start now. After all, very few of her customers would want to let the government in on the fact that they availed themselves of Hortense's services.

Then one balmy evening in late summer a certain satisfied customer of Hortense's gave a recommendation to the wrong person. He turned out to be an IRS special agent who had slipped into the bar that night after a grueling twelve-hour session with an honest taxpayer. He was just itching to uncover a bona fide tax dodger to make up for this setback, and the tip-off from that googoo-eyed stranger reeking of expensive perfume was right on target.

Following the rather complicated directions entrusted to him by Googoo Eyes, the special agent finally arrived at Hortense's House of Pleasure deep in a dark, dense forest, at the end of a twisting, overgrown dirt road. He'd almost turned back several times because of the forbidding surroundings, thinking not enough self-respecting johns would venture this far for a few hours of feminine attention. What kind of bordello would be located in a place like this? he asked himself, picturing some broken-down wooden shack with a leaky roof. But then another answer came to him: ah, yes, the clever kind that doesn't want the government to know about its existence.

It would be a nice place after all, he assured himself, but he still was not prepared for the Xanadu he finally encountered. The eighteen-bedroom palace sprawled invitingly around a softly lit courtyard; leggy girls in satin gowns pandered to the many customers' every whim; there was a large, stocked bar, swimming pools, game rooms, the works; the place was dripping with luxury. Among the many and varied reactions welling up inside the special agent was one overriding word: JACKPOT! Hortense and her employees didn't know it yet, but they would soon join the ranks of American taxpayers. The fact that Hortense's business was outside the law made no difference. As long as it was earning money, Uncle Sam was entitled to his share.

* * *

In their eternal struggle to hide income from the Internal Revenue Service, Americans have devised many ingenious ways to avoid paying taxes. But whenever the IRS finds out about one, they devise methods of their own to prove the existence of that income. If they can't do it with a Source and Application schedule, or a Net Worth or Bank Deposit examination, they still have a few other clever tricks up their sleeves. Even for people who have no records in government files, no bank accounts, no financial books, and who deal exclusively in cash, the IRS has a circumstantial method they can employ. True, they may never be able to determine conclusively that their victim took in the amounts they estimate, but by that time the victim's only recourse is to try to disprove the IRS's contentions. If he can't, he'll be expected to pay the tax that has been conveniently computed for him.

Of course, the Internal Revenue Service doesn't just pull a figure out of the air and claim that's what the errant taxpayer owes them. The agent assigned to the case will take pains to calculate actual income as accurately as possible, using whatever evidence he can gather. In Hortense Bedfiller's case the special agent got a fair idea of her business's income just by looking around. There were the lavishly furnished bedrooms, the jewels dangling from every girl in the house, the eight-car garage filled with brand new Porsches, Mercedes, Rolls-Royces and a golf cart, the works. The source of all those riches was obvious, too, in the form of large denominations of currency being passed from big, hairy hands into soft, delicate ones. By determining the approximate value of the house and its appointments, he could come up with a reasonable estimation of Hortense's income. Or he might choose to keep a tally of the nightly traffic, multiplied by the average fee paid by each customer. Average it out over a one-month period, multiply by twelve, and the annual income emerges.

Further investigation would then be done on the individual employees, yielding more concrete evidence, and perhaps even more taxes. No wonder he'd gotten so excited when he laid eyes on Hortense's House. And they thought he was just feeling amorous!

Since this was to be no ordinary tax investigation, an out-of-the ordinary method of proof was called for. Two seldom-used methods came to mind: 1) Expenditures; and 2) Unit and Volume. The former would show how much Hortense took in by evaluating everything she spent money on, in a procedure similar to Net Worth (see chapter 9). The latter would attempt to determine the approximate number of customers serviced, and the average amount spent by each. Let's look at them one at a time (the methods, not the customers).

EXPENDITURES

By doing a Net Worth report, an IRS agent can prove money came in by showing increases in net worth plus nondeductible expenditures. The key to this method lies in the difference between the taxpayer's net worth at the beginning of the year and the end. However, Hortense spends her money almost as quickly as she rakes it in, so that her net worth at the end of any given year is approximately the same as it was at the beginning. Yet, the way she spends money, it's obvious she has quite a hefty income. How to prove it?

The special agent may start by establishing a beginning net worth, and then listing everything that was spent during the year. The total amount of these expenditures reduced by nontaxable funds represents income. But if the taxpayer deals mostly in cash and has no canceled checks to trace, how can they find out what was spent on what?

Well, Hortense may not keep any financial records, but her merchants do. And since only a limited number of local ones sell the kind of merchandise Hortense is interested in, it's not long before the special agent has tracked them down, along with their copies of Hortense's receipts. From the Rolls-Royce dealer to Aristocracy Jewelers, the IRS agent makes a grand tour of the places Hortense and "family" spread their wealth. Even the bank has a few records from the times they bought bank checks to pay for mail-order underwear and divorce decrees. And of course, the realtor who sold her the house can open a few doors, too. By the time he's finished following in Hortense's diamond-studded footsteps, the special agent has a whole armload of dated records of her expenditures. He may have missed a few, but he'll still have plenty from which to make his calculations.

In Hortense's case the biggest single item listed in her Expenditures statement is "Personal Living Expenses," except for the year she bought the house. Its value was figured into her net worth, as were such additional assets as the furnishings, previously purchased cars, furs, and a dozen or so exotic pets. Other real-estate holdings were uncovered, as were "gifts" from some of the regulars who preferred giving their excess income to Hortense's girls rather than to Uncle Sam. These had to be subtracted, of course, since they are nontaxable items. And once the girls got that through their pretty heads, they began remembering all sorts of gifts men had showered upon them. Then the special agent wanted to know the names of their benefactors . . .

"You mean he was using a phony name? Aw, he seemed like such a nice guy, too. . . ."

Among other assets the IRS will look for when doing an Expenditures statement are: cash—on hand and in bank accounts; inventories; U.S. Savings Bonds; loans repaid; equipment and other business property; loan payments; insurance premiums; and such nontaxable items as inheritances, depreciation, return of capital, and gifts. Appropriate deductions are then subtracted to arrive at unreported taxable income.

One reason a special agent may choose the Expenditures method is its appeal to a jury. When an extravagant life-style can be illustrated in titillating detail, it has a greater impact on those twelve impartial (but not very rich) jurors, who may then convict on the basis of pure jealousy. Put yourself in a jury box and think how you might react to a plea like the following:

"Ms. Bedfiller makes no secret of her wealth, once you make your way to her secluded mansion, filled with glittering splendor from plushly carpeted floors to crystal-chandeliered ceilings. Do not judge her life-style by the unadorned creature in torn blue-jeans you see before you now, but by *this*"—he pulls out a three-foot-long print-out—"well-documented shopping list. I won't take up the court's valuable time reading the entire list of the defendant's purchases, but a few random samples will be enlightening: to Vandergam's Furs: $14,762 for two minks and a seal; Vendorskin's Gems: $24,995 for assorted baubles and bangles; here's a good one—to Noah's Arch: $6,500 for one ostrich, two baboons, and a pregnant ocelot; Transcendental Tours for a deluxe cruise to Antarctica via the South Sea Isles . . ."

And as you picture scantily clad young ladies bedecked in orchids walking their pet ocelots on jewel-encrusted leashes, you think of that $3,000 Uncle Sam carved out of your meager salary, and you do the only fair thing, besides finding out how to get to Hortense's House of Pleasure.

Since case law has established the admissibility of the Expenditures method in court, the IRS need not fear that its evidence will be rejected. However, sometimes one method is not enough, and so they will compute the defendant's income using another method to back up the first. A logical choice is Net Worth, since its starting point is the same as for Expenditures. It also has the advantage of demonstrating that the income could not have come from sale of assets, since the ending net worth will show that the assets were still on hand. In any case, for criminal prosecution, the IRS must offer the same kind of evidence—a likely source of income must be established, or nontaxable income negated—or the case probably won't stand up.

UNIT AND VOLUME

Even rarer than the Expenditures method of proving income is Unit and Volume. In a case like Hortense Bedfiller's, it could be useful, particularly if the IRS keeps its initial investigation a secret. In order to do a Unit and Volume report, two things must be known: 1) the number of units handled by the taxpayer (that is, customers) and 2) the price charged for each. And chances are if Hortense knew they were investigating her, she'd see to it that they wouldn't be able to determine those figures. She would simply pack her girls off on an extended holiday and set up shop elsewhere.

Once the special agent has confirmed his suspicions that Hortense is not paying her taxes, he might pose as a "regular" for a week or so—long enough to establish the average number of customers who patronize the place per week. That gives him his "volume" figure. And Hortense has graciously supplied a price list for her various services which amount to five basic charges ranging from a fifteen-minute quickie to an all-night, all-out adventure. That gives him his "units" figure. The IRS agent has merely to figure out the proportion of customers utilizing each service, do a little multiplication, and make his presence known to the unsuspecting madame, who will wonder how in the world this guy found out how much money she's been making.

Elementary, he replies. I used Unit and Volume. This method may also be appropriate for regulated businesses like funeral homes or realtors, who must report each transaction to a department of a city government. The department can then supply the number of customers the taxpayer in question dealt with, and his income can be derived from this figure. Garment manufacturers employing union laborers can be uncovered this way, by finding out how many union labels were purchased by their plants. Any producer who pays on a piecework basis may be the subject of a Unit and Volume investigation, if no other method seems feasible. Tax courts have upheld it as a valid method of proof. Its use is justified by the taxpayer's own failure to keep adequate records or file a proper return. In criminal cases it would probably not be accepted as prima facie evidence, but it could be used to back up another method.

If the IRS cannot prove your income using a method like Net Worth or Bank Deposits, they will attempt to bring it to light some other way. They may use the Expenditures method, a cousin of Net Worth, which treats everything you purchased above your beginning net worth as income. If that doesn't work, they may, on rare occasions, do a Unit and Volume, by multiplying the number of units you sold by the average price you sold them for. This works especially well when the goods or services are relatively few in variety, and the price is stable. Any business done on a piecework basis would lend itself to a Unit and Volume investigation. Hortense's House of Pleasure is a prime example. After selling a few of the

Rolls-Royces and furs to pay her taxes, Hortense has taken a course in accounting so she can keep her new ledgers straight, and she now insists on screening every new customer carefully before allowing him admittance.

The following chapter contains still more indirect methods the IRS has at its disposal. Face it, if they can't get you one way, they'll think of another.

CHAPTER 13

More Indirect Methods

So far you have read about five indirect methods the IRS has available to prove gross income for tax purposes. With all that artillery going for them, perhaps you think the only way for a tax dodger to avoid being assessed for additional taxes is somehow to avoid being noticed by IRS. Perhaps you're right. In addition to the previously covered methods there are still others they can use to get the evidence they're after. As if Net Worth, Bank Deposits, Source and Application, Expenditures, and Unit and Volume weren't enough, they may decide to use one of two other methods on you, just because it will be easier to manage under the circumstances. One is called Cash "T" (for transactions, and the way the schedule is arranged); the second, which is not often used, is known as Percentages. As with the other methods, they will be looking for income you may not have reported on your tax return, and they will hope it's taxable, so they can help themselves to some of it.

When a revenue agent or auditor faces a new case, he mentally flips through the arsenal of methods he can use to determine which is the best one for this particular case. If everything seems pretty straightforward and ordinary, he may do a quick Source and Application schedule, subtracting sources from applications of funds to find out if the taxpayer spent more than he took in; he may assume the difference to be unreported income. He could reach a similar conclusion using a Net Worth, only he will arrive at it via different channels: First, establish a starting point for the beginning of the year consisting of assets minus liabilities; subtract that from end-of-the-year net worth, add in nondeductible expenditures, and see if the total agrees with what the taxpayer reported. Or he might be able to find a difference through Bank Deposits, using bank and brokerage records as a basis for the calculation. Maybe this taxpayer has such a lavish life-style, he cries out for an Expenditures investigation, wherein dollar values for the year's purchases are added together to prove the taxpayer was spending money, which must have been income. Or perhaps it would be an easy matter to establish the amount of business the taxpayer did by multiplying the number of units sold at the price he's been charging for each. That garment maker who pays on a piecework basis is an ideal candidate for the Unit and Volume method.

Well, for one reason or another, this revenue agent has ruled out all five of these methods. Maybe his group manager favors the Cash "T," which means it is used ninety-nine percent of the time in that particular group. Or maybe your dealings just naturally seem to gravitate toward that kind of division, or the agent has grown very fond of this one method and has done it so often he's almost forgotten how to use the others. Well, whatever the reason, the decision has been made. When you see what appears to be a huge letter "T" boldly drawn down the page in front of the tax man, brace yourself. He's about to do a Cash "T" on you.

CASH "T"

If anyone is going to do a Cash "T," it will most probably be someone from IRS's Examination Division: a revenue agent or an auditor. Special agents hardly ever use it, except as verification or to make rapid determinations of possible unreported income, just to see if you warrant their time.

It is the speed factor which makes Cash "T," like Source and Application, a desirable method of proof. It has other similarities to Source and Application as well. In both types money is divided into two main categories: what you took in, and what you paid out. Only this time the applications are called "credits" and sources are labeled "debits." And, while "Sources" are situated beneath "Applications" on the Source and Application form, the Cash "T" 's debits and credits are usually listed side by side—debits on the left, credits on the right. The difference between debits and credits is then computed to determine any unreported income.

Cash "T" is so much like the Source and Application method, it's sometimes difficult to tell them apart. Actually Cash "T" is more consistent with the true theory of "source and application" than the Source and Application form used by IRS. The chief difference between the two lies in the way they categorize your income. Where a Source and Application form subtracts net profits and depreciation from inventory increases, Cash "T" concentrates on actual moneys paid out, such as purchases and operating expenses. It does not lend itself to cost of goods sold, inventories, or depreciation, as does Source and Application. The latter is a shortcut method for computing the same difference between income and outlays as that generated by Cash "T." But basically, one is about as fast as the other.

Cash "T" operates on the premise that all types of income and expenditures are "cash transactions" flowing into and out of a cash account expressed as double-entry accounting records. Even if you pay for everything by check or with your Handy Dandy charge card, they're going to pretend it was all cash so they can get it over with quickly. A typical Cash "T" account might contain the following items:

Debits (available funds)	Credits (paid out)
Cash on hand, 1-1	Cash on hand, 12-31
Savings, 1-1	Savings, 12-31
Checking, personal, 1-1	Checking, personal 12-31
Checking, business, 1-1	Checking, business, 12-31
Loan proceeds	Loan payments, less interest*
Interest income	Equipment purchases
Prior year state tax refund	Installment payments, less interest*
Schedule _____ receipts	
Wages less withholding tax	Purchases (per return)
Dividends (including deductible portion)	Other expenses, except depreciation (per return)

Sales of assets (gross sale price)

Rent receipts

Nontaxable income (gifts, prior year federal income tax refund, etc.)

Rent expense, less depreciation expenses

Schedule _____ expenses

Personal living expenses

* Interest may be accounted for in "other expenses except depreciation, per return," or "personal living expenses."

For taxpayers who deal on accrual rather than cash basis, certain adjustments must be made. In the case of Accounts Receivable, the beginning balance is just like cash on hand, since, like an IOU, it can be converted to cash. Therefore it is listed as "Debits," or source, on the Cash "T." The ending balance indicates what you applied some of your inventory toward (such as a promise to pay) so that makes it a "Credit." Accounts Payable works in reverse. The beginning balance represents money to be applied at some future date, so it's entered as a "Credit" (application). If Accounts Payable totaled $3,000 at the beginning of the year and zero at the end, it means you applied $3,000 sometime during the year to pay off your creditors. The ending balance of Accounts Payable indicates expenses deducted but not yet paid; since these funds were theoretically available as a source for other expenditures, they are listed as a "Debit" on Cash "T." Some agents may dispense with listing beginning and ending balances by simply entering decreases in Accounts Receivable and increases in Accounts Payable as "Debits," and just the opposite on the "Credits" side. Either way the end result will be the same. Got it? Read it again slowly, you'll catch on soon. If you're on a cash basis, forget this whole paragraph. It doesn't apply to you.

Once the tax man has amassed all your sources and ap—er, make that "debits" and "credits," he must be careful to steer clear of the same mistakes he can encounter with the other methods of computing income (as discussed in Chapters 10 and 11). For instance, he's got to be sure he hasn't duplicated any expenses, like the interest on loans or deductible portions of insurance policies. And if you've taken your deduction for dividends on your return, this excluded part should be added in with all of your cash-paid dividends under "Debits"; otherwise, credits may erroneously exceed debits by this amount. However, a stock dividend should not be included, since it was not available to spend. Again, bank-account balances must be reconciled at both ends of the year, and cash on hand should be firmly established. A good revenue agent knows all this, of course, but it wouldn't hurt to keep an eye on him, just in case.

When he gets around to adding each side of the "T" together, you're going to hope they come out as close to equal as possible. If the total credits turn out to exceed total debits by any significant amount, he'll assume the difference to be a tentative understatement of income. He'll be very curious to hear your explanation for this, because if you don't have a good one, he'll see to it that you get your very own invoice from the U.S. Treasury requesting the presence of your money at its next National Budget Bash.

On the other hand, you could have a very good explanation for the apparent discrepancy. Scanning the list of figures, you might suddenly remember some other income you forgot to report—that tax-free $50,000 you inherited from your late ex-wife, perhaps, or that old bedroom furniture you sold last January; or maybe you really didn't spend as much as he thinks you did. It could be as simple as a mathematical error—you hope, as the agent adds the columns for the fourteenth time. If you can't think of a good explanation—mainly because there isn't one— you may as well just resign yourself to paying the additional taxes they'll be assessing, unless you want to go through a lengthy court battle that could wind up costing more than the government wanted from you. Of course, if a large enough discrepancy is found, *they* may take *you* to court. But whether it's large or small, they'll want to know why you didn't report the difference. Well-ll, deep down, they *know* why, but they like to hear you admit it. In another era people like that could be found in confession booths.

You may think you're safe if debits turn out higher than credits. Think again. If debits far exceed credits, it means there must be some expenditures you did not account for. At this point the tax man may very well wonder what else you might be hiding—income from a hidden business, perhaps? Gambling winnings? Your autographed photo of Howard Jarvis? This may be a good time to wipe the egg off your flushed face, or disengage the foot that somehow found its way to your gaping mouth. The answer you might give to the agent's inquiry is known in some IRS circles as the "ah-buh." That is often the extent of the vocabulary of a taxpayer caught with excess debits showing. Some taxpayers offer such clever explanations as "I guess I spent more for clothes or food than I thought, heh-heh-heh."

PERCENTAGES

Thousands of tax investigations take place each year, but only a small percentage of them will employ the Percentages method of proof. Even so, you should know a little about it, on the off chance that they decide to dust it off when they get to your case.

Actually, when the Percentages method is used at all, it's often in conjunction with some other method—one of the six we have covered so far. It is sometimes helpful (to the IRS, not you) in evaluating allegations from informants regarding such juicy gossip as other people's unreported profits or income. There have been a few isolated cases in which tax courts have accepted Percentages evidence by itself, but, for the most part, both civil and criminal courts require more substantial proof.

The reason is that, of all the indirect methods, Percentages is the most circumstantial. The agent using it may not even do a direct evaluation of the income in question, because he cannot get to it—the taxpayer may have been uncooperative. So the agent turns to another business in the community of a similar nature, where he will find inventories, sales, and profits that roughly approximate the prime target's. If the suspect is a restaurant popular with the teeny-bopper crowd, he'll look for another such fast-food establishment with about the same amount of volume and business, in the same general area, with about the same number of employees. Unless he chances upon a fluke, he won't get an exact match, but he'll try to get as close as possible. To be really fair, he may seek out several other similar restaurants, and average them all together.

The reference restaurants may begin to think they're the ones under investigation, as the tax man goes through their books to determine the percentages he's after. He is looking for ratios: how various expenses relate to gross sales, including the percentage of sales that normally wind up as net profits. Some items will be easier to figure out than others: The wholesale cost of food, for instance, can be traced back to suppliers in the area, who may also supply volume figures for each eatery. There may be a slight variation in wage scales, but it shouldn't be much. After going over the other restaurants' figures, the tax man might come up with something like this:

Gross sales	$100,000
% to salaries	20%
% to supplies	10%
% to food, beverages	25%
% to other expenses	15%
Net Profit	30%, or $30,000

Now, if he can get a firm figure on any one of the expenses paid out by the taxpayer under investigation, the tax man need only divide that amount by the percentage established for that particular expense to determine approximate gross sales. He would then multiply that by the "Net Profit" percentage. For example, a check with local food and beverage suppliers indicated that Teeny Bopper's Eat-in purchased $50,000 worth of their merchandise for the year under investigation. The agent knows that a typical teeny-bopper restaurant in that locale spends twenty-five percent of its gross income on this expense. Dividing this percentage into the $50,000 yields gross sales of about $200,000. If Teeny Bopper's Eat-in is like the other restaurants, its Net Profit was about thirty percent of that, or $60,000.

The basis for most of these calculations came from outside Teeny Bopper's, but some of the information could have come straight from the horse's mouth—whatever the owner was willing to tell him. The menu contained a handy reference to retail prices. Some employees may have divulged their salaries, and anything they knew of the boss's spending habits. If any adjustments are necessary, the tax man will make them; then he'll compare the average percentages with Teeny Bopper's, which will give him a rough idea of its income.

"Thirty percent profits???" cries a stunned owner when confronted with the evidence. "I should live so long! Tell me another good one."

So the agent tells him he wouldn't have had to use such a roundabout method if the owner had kept accurate records and cooperated with him in the first place.

The Percentages method does have its drawbacks. Even in this age of conformity, it's hard to find two businesses sufficiently alike to compare. It would hardly do to compare the independently owned general store with the giant Food-o-Rama in the shopping center. Nor would they try to compare it with a hardware store, or any other establishment that sells different kinds of merchandise. Prices should be similar, too, since some stores mark up their merchandise higher than others. Location can also make a difference: A big-city drugstore's profits can be miles removed from one situated in a small town. And, to account for inflation, they'll be sure the periods covered are the same as well. Any significant variation in size, type, merchandising policy, location, or period could render a Percentages calculation practically useless.

A more objective approach is when the IRS agent concentrates on your business alone. To arrive at your gross sales, he contacts your suppliers, determines how much you purchased, then applies your percentage mark-up to these amounts. Of course, this may not take into consideration such things as red-tag sales, inventory spoilage, shoplifting, and so on. So it may paint an unreliable picture of your finances. No wonder the Percentages method isn't used very much.

Net Worth, Bank Deposits, Source and Application, Expenditures, Unit and Volume, Cash "T," Percentages—the Internal Revenue Service is armed with almost as many different kinds of weapons as the military services. And those are just *indirect* methods; wait till you see how special agents use Specific Items ...

Are you beginning to feel weak, defenseless, paranoid, in the face of such intimidating odds? Well, your best defense is a complete and accurate set of financial records kept in a contemporaneous manner.

Then, if you reported all the income you were supposed to, an IRS investigation should simply confirm that fact. And if not—well, now you can contemplate which method they might use on you. Sorry, no tax breaks for guessing right.

CHAPTER 14

Go Directly to Jail!

SPECIFIC ITEMS II: CRIMINAL

ITEM: Rodney Rotgut earned $456,789 from his distillery last year.

ITEM: Rodney also got lucky at the track, yielding an additional $32,000 in income.

ITEM: What he did not spend on high living and low profiles went into Rodney's Swiss bank account or to support his ailing mother in the style she had become accustomed to.

ITEM: The IRS thinks Rodney owes them more than the $1,200 he paid them in taxes. The IRS, as usual, is right.

ITEM: Rodney Rotgut is in for trouble.

Now that Rodney has come to the attention of the IRS Criminal Investigation Division, their task is to break these generally known facts down into specifics, if possible, to prove Rodney had more taxable income than he reported. Instead of trying to prove their allegations through one of the indirect methods, this time they decide to delve directly into Rodney's dealings to identify the specific amounts of income he received, and where each amount came from. No side-door entrances for Rodney; for him, they will bypass those less reliable indirect methods and get right down to Specific Items.

As employed by the Criminal Investigation Division, the Specific Items method of proving income consists of a list of how much you took in for what, and how much you spent on what. Since it involves a thorough examination of your accounts for the entire tax period under investigation, it can be a very time-consuming process, especially if you have a lot of customers or clients in far-flung locations. But it may be the only way the IRS can get the evidence they must have in order to prove additional taxes. Where a federal district court may doubt a Bank Deposits or an Expenditures report as too circumstantial, it would be difficult to discount a concrete, documented list of the actual moneys you collected and applied during the year. Thus it is the preferred method of proof for special agents conducting criminal investigations, since it contains the most convincing evidence they can present to a jury.

Chapter 8 has already outlined the ways in which Specific Items is used by the civil authorities. In most cases tax examiners will simply choose a few questionable deductions on your tax return and ask you to bring in proof of them. But when a criminal investigator gets in on the act, the number of specific items he'll be looking for increases dramatically.

When a special agent employs the Specific Items method, there are two main directions he can go, besides in and out. He will either:

1) find each specific item of unreported income, or
2) compare what you *should* have reported with what you did report on your income-tax return. This is known in some IRS circles as "overfilling the bucket," the bucket being reported income, the overflow representing additional income.

Whichever path he chooses, his ultimate quarry remains: What came in from where, what was it for, and when did you receive it?

By the time your case is referred to the Criminal Investigation Division, the IRS is usually reasonably sure you had some income you didn't tell them about. It is that unreported income a special agent is out to uncover. Whether he decides to locate specific unreported items or overfill the bucket, he is going to contact your clients or customers—anyone who paid you anything—and ask each the same basic questions:

"Did Mr. Taxpayer sell you any of his merchandise (or services) last year? How much did you pay him? Thankyouverymuch. Next!"

These witnesses are usually requested to present a receipt or canceled check as positive proof of the date and amount of business they did with you, and swear to their statements in writing. But sometimes their testimony alone is sufficient.

The more customers' testimonies he can procure, the more conclusive his evidence will be. If possible he will contact every one of them. But if you have more than a couple of hundred of them, it could take longer than the agent wishes to spend to garner each individual testimony. Or some of your clients may have moved, died, or otherwise become misplaced, making contact improbable, if not impossible. In such a case the agent may simply contact a certain percentage of them, say thirty or fifty percent, to verify your own records. He might start by sending out invitations to every name on your ledger, requesting the honor of their presence at the IRS office. Maybe half of these will show up, either to confirm or refute the amount your books claimed they paid you. If most or all of these random samplings of customers affirm your figures, the special agent may assume that your books are correct, and record his findings accordingly.

Once he has gathered your clients' testimonies, the special agent will compare what they told him with what you told the IRS on your tax return. If there is an understatement, he now has reasonable proof of it. His next step, if he can feasibly do it, is to try to find out which specific checks or items of income you did not report. Looking over your return and schedules, he'll locate the ones you did report; any that are left over account for specific items of unreported income. Or, if he could not prove each specific item you failed to report, at least he has the difference between what you did report and what you should have reported. To make sure the unreported income didn't go for additional deductible expenditures you may claim later on, he will now attempt to prove what you did with the unreported income.

Once again, like the guy in the middle of the highway, he can take two directions in the search for his proof:

1) prove where each specific item of unreported income went; or

2) use an indirect method to show that total non-deductible applications of funds exceeded reported income by at least the amount he has determined to be unreported income.

This second approach is taken when they cannot trace each specific item, for one reason or another. Perhaps you dealt mostly in cash. Then the agent might do a Source and Application or an Expenditures schedule which will show that you spent more than you reported, and that the difference in income could not have gone toward unreported business expenses; instead, the money was used for personal living expenses or to increase your net worth. Whichever indirect method the agent chooses, it will not only show how these items were disbursed, but it will also help to back up the amounts he has already proved to be unreported income. Of course, if possible, he'll try to be as specific with outlays as he was with income.

There are a number of places an IRS agent can look as he starts tracking down your expenditures. Where could that money have gone? he asks himself. One thing he knows for sure: It never reached the U.S. Treasury. So he begins tracing it through any records or leads you may have supplied—banks, brokerage houses, friends, relatives, employees, anyone who might know. Along the way some ver-rr-ry interesting clues could turn up.

"Why would a person who lives in a townhouse keep making odd payments to Tricky Tractor Repair Service?" the agent might ask himself, having no one else to talk to. The answer could turn up a few more leads—such as a two-hundred-acre soybean plantation the suspect neglected to tell IRS about.

Bank accounts figure significantly in just about every IRS criminal investigation. As in the Bank Deposits indirect method, a sampling of your deposits can give a fairly good indication of your income. Some of them might correspond directly with some of those unreported checks the special agent is trying to trace. But what about those secret accounts you've been hiding from the government so they couldn't tax it? Here is where third parties can be most helpful to an IRS agent. Your former bookkeeper, dissatisfied customers, business partner, return preparer, maybe even your spouse, could shed some awfully bright light on your case, pointing the way not only to those hidden funds, but to other juicy little tidbits as well.

"Well, if there was nothing left in your joint account," he inquires of your wife, "where did he get the money for your son's new car?"

Your faithful spouse may cover for you with a viable explanation, but if she's your *ex*-wife, watch out . . . especially if she's not happy with the alimony settlement, or you're eight months behind on your payments. Special agents love disgruntled former spouses and associates. Sometimes these grudge-bearers even come forward on their own to inform on delinquent taxpayers.

"All I know is, he doesn't spend his money on me," pouts the cloistered wife from the pay phone. "I'd rather see it go to the government than that floozie of his."

And of course, the IRS will be as happy to oblige

the lovelorn wife as she is to inform on her husband. The point is, it's not only your customers who will figure as witnesses in an IRS investigation; anyone who might know something about your dealings is fair game. Rodney Rotgut's bookie, for example, became very talkative when the IRS assured him that *he* was not under investigation at that time. Result: a full accounting of every win, place, and show Rodney's money was riding on.

Like so many other taxpayers with a criminal investigator on their tails, Rodney tried to claim more expenses than he had originally claimed on his tax return. On and on he droned about labor problems, transportation costs, skyrocketing fuel bills, and too many employees sampling the product. Since Rodney's was a criminal case, it was up to the special agent to prove that Rodney could not have incurred all the expenses he was claiming, because he knew that somewhere during the trial, someone was going to want to know how he could be so sure Rodney's claims were false.

Up to the witness stand steps the president of Triple Trucking Company, who has already sworn to the agent in a signed affidavit that Mr. Rotgut paid his firm a total of $14,000 during the year in question. Now he repeats that testimony for the benefit of the jury, exchanging meaningful glances with the special agent who's absently fiddling with the affidavit a few feet away.

Next witness: the special agent himself. "Although Mr. Rotgut claimed he spent $27,000 for transportation costs that year," he begins confidently, "he told me during repeated interviews that Triple Trucking

Company was the only transporter he used." Rodney starts squirming, perspiring, and wishing he were somewhere else.

"During my investigation," the agent continues, "I could find no transporter that Mr. Rotgut used other than Triple Trucking, nor any records indicating that Rotgut's Distillery paid Triple Trucking more than the $14,000 they testified to." Rodney is visibly disturbed as the agent testifies that $13,000 was spent on a luxury cruise for the entire Rotgut family, not for business expenses. Rodney is itching to say something—anything—to defend himself, but is restrained by a sharp tug on his coattails from his attorney.

A special agent's court testimony could go far toward convicting a defendant. He is usually the government's key third-party witness; his courtroom role is also that of technical assistant for the government attorney. He will present documents (or certified copies of them) which the taxpayer previously supplied to him, and he can also repeat statements or admissions the taxpayer may have made to him during interviews. He will give summaries of his findings, too.

For certain important evidence some of the witnesses the agent contacted during his investigation may be called on to repeat their testimony in court. Often, however, the defense will have reviewed witnesses' statements before the trial begins, and stipulated its acceptance of some of them, thereby hastening the proceedings.

Up to this point we have been discussing how the Specific Items method can prove unreported income. But what if the taxpayer did report his income correctly, but cheated the government of its share by overstating his expenses? It has happened, and Specific Items has been able to uncover such a ruse. Where an indirect method will automatically arrive at the discrepancy as just additional taxable income, without identifying it as unreported income or overstated expenses, the direct method goes a step further. Once a special agent has concluded that reported income was correct, he will take a closer look at the taxpayer's expenses, since he knows the discrepancy has to be accounted for somewhere. He might uncover a pattern, say a twenty percent overstatement on each expense, which the taxpayer deducted consistently, right down the line. The more altered documents and falsified records he can find, the more intent will be evident for criminal purposes, whether the pattern was consistent or not. For example, the taxpayer may have made $100,000 gross sales; of that, $70,000 went for expenses. But instead of reporting his net income as $30,000, the correct figure, he reported expenses of $80,000, leaving him only a $20,000 net profit. An auditor does an indirect method on him, listing the $80,000 in claimed business expenses plus $30,000 in personal living expenses. "Gosh!" the auditor says to himself, "that makes $110,000 in applications . . . $10,000 more than he reported for gross sales!" When a special agent is called in on the case, he questions the auditor about his suspicions, leading the special agent down a trail of the taxpayer's business expenses. Soon the specific expense items that were overstated emerge.

In most cases only those specific items that can be proved beyond a reasonable doubt will be entered as evidence in a criminal case; for, when the government brings criminal charges against a taxpayer, the burden of proof is on them. Thus the understatement claimed in a criminal case is likely to be lower than civil authorities say it is, since the latter do not have as heavy a burden to prove their computations for additional taxes. Where a special agent will usually give you the benefit of the doubt when questionable income is involved, a revenue agent is more inclined to count it as additional taxable income, since all he needs is some adequate grounds for belief, such as your inability to prove certain income was nontaxable.

"But I told you a hundred times," screams the taxpayer in frustration, "that four thousand dollars was just the loan my late uncle repaid me, after two years!"

"Prove it," the revenue agent says smugly. If you can't, you may very well have to pay taxes on it.

The same situation can apply to deductions. While a special agent might let them go for criminal purposes, the Examination Division is more inclined to disallow a specific deduction if you don't have adequate documentation.

Since it is more conclusive than the seven indirect methods of proving income covered in preceding chapters, the Specific Items method is the preferred procedure for criminal cases. Civil authorities use it, too, but they don't go into as much detail as criminal investigators. In seeking to identify exactly how much you took in and paid out, the IRS agent may either 1) find each specific item of unreported income or 2) compare what you *should* have reported with what you did report (overfill the bucket). In tracing income, he will contact all of your customers or clients, or thirty to fifty percent of them, and find out how much each paid you. He will then attempt to prove where these specific items of unreported income went; if that is not possible, he'll use an indirect method to prove your total expenditures exceeded what you reported you had available to spend. Since the burden of proof is on the government in criminal cases, they will probably claim less unreported income than will civil authorities. The latter will be more inclined to retain a higher amount of unreported income, leaving you to prove otherwise. And the following chapter just might give you some ideas on how to do this.

CHAPTER 15

Income Cracks:
How Their Proof
Can Fall Apart

Nobody's perfect, as anyone acquainted with the human condition knows; and that includes the Internal Revenue Service. They would like nothing better than a foolproof method of proving income that could pass every test beyond the shadow of a doubt. Unfortunately for them (and fortunately for you), every method we have discussed herein contains a number of built-in imperfections. From the obvious shortcomings of the Percentages indirect method to the camouflaged traps beneath the surface of Source and Application, there is always something that can throw off a tax man's calculations, no matter how carefully he arrives at his results. Even the most reliable method, Specific Items, has its problems, such as incorrect inventories.

If an error does show up after the IRS has examined your dealings, they could point that accusing finger at you for not providing all the information they needed to produce a correct report. But then, you can't be expected to know the intricate workings of IRS methodology—not even after digesting this informative, but limited, book. If they wanted the information, you argue, they should have asked for it—in terms you could understand. And that is a perfectly valid argument, too. Indeed, it has caused more than one case to be turned around. On the other hand, more than a few taxpayers have simply gritted their teeth and paid the additional taxes the IRS assessed, not daring to defy the Word from On High. If they had only taken the trouble to learn a little about the places an Internal Revenue Service investigation could go off track, they might have spotted some errors that could have saved them a bundle. First, they must admit to themselves that even the mighty IRS can make mistakes, despite their vast knowledge and experience. You, dear reader, have already recognized that fact, haven't you? For your wisdom and foresight, you are to be congratulated . . . and rewarded—with this chapter, dealing with IRS mistakes you might otherwise have missed.

Ordinarily the IRS will hold you responsible for your own tax return. However, when it comes to criminal cases, you may be able to point the finger at someone else, since special agents must firmly establish the responsibility for the filing and accuracy of tax returns under their scrutiny. Some taxpayers have successfully shifted the blame for fraudulent acts onto their accountants or spouses, after taking a closer look at their miscalculated returns. However, as you already know, you are the one who is ultimately responsible for paying your correct tax.

While each method of proving income has its own peculiar idiosyncracies that may throw it off, there are some basic defects common to all of them. For instance, if the investigation covers a period rapidly receding into history (more than three years ago in some cases), pertinent records could have been lost or destroyed, key witnesses may not be available, or you simply might have forgotten facts relevant to your case. After all, nobody's perfect, you know. The tax man certainly knows it, but he often seems to come out more perfect than the taxpayer he's investigating. While he doesn't necessarily hope you are unaware of his methods, it's still easier for him to operate from a position of invincibility. "I'm less likely to be challenged if the ignorant taxpayer thinks I know it all," he deduces. And speaking of deductions, he's just spotted another one you shouldn't have taken. Zap! There it goes, with one swift stroke of his pen.

Well, he may be able to pull that with other taxpayers, but not you. You're armed: You know what can be deducted and what can't, and soon you are overwhelming him with your knowledge of tax matters. You admit that you did have additional income, but had no compulsion to report it since it was nontaxable anyway. You then produce documents to prove it. Or you prove that additional income he's getting so excited about was just accumulation from a prior year. And you know perfectly well that cash on hand at the beginning of the year constitutes nontaxable money for that year. Oh, yes, this tax man has met his match in you. After years of intimidating those meek, cowering, guilt-ridden taxpayers, he's getting a dose of his own medicine. Good for you! He was beginning to get a superiority complex anyway. Don't get carried away, though, or you might just boast your way right into a trap. An overt display of your knowledge of tax matters can be used as intent in a criminal case against you.

On the other hand, the fault may lie with the tax man himself, especially if he's conducting a criminal investigation. Sometimes it can be advantageous to learn something about the number of years he's been employed by IRS, his manner of questioning, his interpretation of answers, and how your return came to the examiner from the time it left the regional Service Center. This type of information could be most useful to professionals experienced in preparing defenses for tax cases, especially criminal cases. For the average taxpayer, though, the main things to look for are defects in the methods of proving income, rather than in the people who employ them. Some of the specifics to be covered herein have been hinted at in previous chapters on direct and indirect methods. For convenience they have been consolidated into a handy checklist (sort of like a Source and Application form).

CASH ON HAND

By now you realize that "cash on hand," in the sense the IRS uses it, is more than just money you happened to have in your pocket. It represents any currency or coins, undeposited checks, legal tender, bank notes or drafts, bank-deposit certificates, commercial paper, money orders, warrants, scrip—anything readily convertible to cash not on deposit in your checking or savings accounts. Cash on hand also includes cash in your safety deposit box. That IOU from your prodigal brother that you use as a bookmark for your Encyclopedia of Trivia; those church bonds that you relegated to a closet shelf and forgot about; the fifty-dollar check from rich Uncle Alfred that you found among your old Christmas cards and finally spent on that sequined lasso you always wanted . . . such easy-to-forget items as these can be considered cash on hand. Even a coin collection can, although it borders on a personal asset when it comes to fixing a value for it. Is that 1901 S limited-edition penny really only worth one cent, its face value? Not to you; that one coin may have a market value of hundreds of dollars. But what did you pay for it? That is what you should give as its value; giving its current (or recent past) market value will artificially increase your net worth although you added no new coins to your collection—that is, assuming the value of collectible coins is keeping pace with inflation.

Why is it so important to include every penny of cash on hand you can? Think back to the ways the IRS goes about proving your income: Using indirect methods, they will account for your expenditures during the year in question. And they will consider whatever you paid out in excess of your sources to be unreported taxable income, which you must be able to explain. If you can't, they may tax it. The explanation, though you may have overlooked it, could lie in a decrease in cash on hand from the beginning of the year to the end. It may be very difficult to remember where you got the money for all your expenditures two or more years ago, but if it was from cash on hand, it would be worth your while to search your memory far and wide, because they can't tax cash you already had on hand, since it can't be construed as income for that year. It may affect the previous year's return, if you forgot about it then, too, but for now they're only investigating last year, not the year the money was received.

Busy as he is, the IRS agent will probably press you for an answer to his "cash on hand" question during the first interview, so he can proceed with the investigation. In fact, you may feel rushed on *every* question, except, perhaps, "How are you?" Sensing his urgency and not wishing to hinder him, you blurt out approximately what he expected to hear: "Oh," you shrug, "I never keep more than a hundred dollars on hand for spending money." It didn't seem that important anyhow. But it *is* that important. If you honestly can't remember how much cash you had on hand at the beginning of the year, don't let him push you into a response that may be too low. If necessary wait until he's finished with you, and then go back and make a careful search of your records; then phone him the answer he was so anxious for. It might mean he'll have to start calculating your income all over again, but that's what he gets for springing such difficult questions on you on the spur of the moment.

If you gave the agent a beginning-of-the-year cash-on-hand estimate that turned out to be too high, he will readily accept the lower figure you give him later. After all, it means he can recommend so much more in taxes. But if your new figure is higher, he's going to want some kind of proof. You're not likely, of course, to have any now—the cash has long since been spent. The tax man knows that cash on hand is a hard item to prove, and so will probably accept the first figure you give him without question (unless it's

213

extremely unreasonable). Thus, it's better to err on the higher side when he first questions you, since it's easier to revise the figure downward later on.

It's not only cash on hand you can bring to his attention after the interview, either; anything bearing on your financial affairs that would help explain discrepancies should be brought to the IRS's attention, no matter how long ago contact was made—assuming they're still working on your case, of course. If they couldn't pin you down on cash on hand, your case may have been dropped.

When the IRS first contacts you, though, your natural reaction might resemble that of a recluse suddenly discovered by the relentless media. The nervousness you feel is understandable, especially if you get one of those examiners who come on like the Spanish Inquisition. "Confess to your sins!" they seem to thunder, wielding their pens like scepters. "Repent or face eternal taxation!"

Faced with such an accusatory personage, you feel every word that comes out of your mouth will help seal your own doom. The Fifth Amendment looks like a possible shelter, but then they might overlook some evidence that *is* in your favor, that only you could have provided. And if you don't tell all, they'll assume the worst! O Lord, why me? you whisper.

"Because . . . you were there!" answers the mighty tax man.

Well, remember, he's just an ordinary mortal who took a course in Indirect Methods, and he can't read your mind. So don't be afraid to tell him about the cash you had on hand in January and spent in May, because since you earned it in a prior year it is nontaxable the year in which you spent it, and will help explain some of your expenditures. The IRS is very meticulous about picking up your transactions from the earliest possible moment: 12:00:01 A.M., January first. Happy New Year! If you paid Aunt Sarah's Caterers $300 for that New Year's breakfast with the money you got in your Christmas stocking, you may have to fork over another $90 to Uncle Sam for it if you don't report the source of that payment. Remember, they'll be listing *all* your expenditures, from January first on.

An underestimated cash-on-hand statement could throw off both indirect and direct methods. In the latter case a decrease may have been used to pay some deductible expense that you forgot to list on your tax return. Of course, an increase in cash on hand from January to December has just the opposite effect: It implies you received money from somewhere to increase your holdings. The IRS, in their infinite curiosity, will want to know where it came from. And if you've learned anything from this book, you'll have a perfectly logical answer all ready to shoot back.

INVENTORIES

If you have a business, you know what a headache it can be to keep track of inventories. But no matter how much aspirin you take for it, the IRS expects you to report inventories as factually as you do the rest of your income. These fluctuations have the same effect as cash on hand when it comes to proving your income. That is, an increase usually means additional income had to have come in to pay for it; a decrease does just the opposite: It usually has the same effect as a nontaxable source of funds. And if you traded an asset, like your used delivery van, for inventories, then you need to point out that particular source of payment, since return of capital on that asset may not be taxable.

If after they've done, say, a Source and Application schedule on you, it turns out your applications of funds exceeded sources, the culprit could be an error in inventories. After all, everything else seems to be in order. So you turn your file cabinets upside down trying to locate the mistake, but all you ever find are rows and rows of those neat little check marks your bookkeeper makes when the end of the month rolls around. You're about to give up and pay the extra tax, when, late one night, as you stare blankly at your routed file cabinets, a small, crumpled paper sticking out from behind one of the cabinets catches your eye. You start to throw it in the trash, but then—hark! A misplaced inventory sheet—for the beginning of that year—with *no check mark on it!*

"Eureka!" you bellow, as if you'd just struck a gold vacuum cleaner. Your inventory figure was too low after all. And now you have proof. That should put those figures back in line.

It does alter the beginning-of-the-year figure, but what does it do to the end of the previous year, which had been brought forward to the year in question? Well, if you had more beginning inventory than you thought, it means you also had more on hand at the end of the previous year. That means the taxes you paid this year may have been too high, but you should have paid more to cover the additional profits you made the previous year. They may then go back to the previous year's return and adjust it accordingly. For example, if your ending inventory for the previous year is changed to a higher figure, it decreases your cost-of-goods-sold expense, and therefore increases your profits by the same amount for that year. So, even though you got a tax break for one year, you wind up paying more for the previous year. In other words, a change in inventories one year has to affect another. As with the size-eighteen lady trying to squeeze into a size-fourteen girdle, the difference has to pop out somewhere. Of course, purchases could have been off, or you may have had an inventory loss somewhere along the line—there could be any number of viable explanations for the discrepancy. If you can't come up with one, though, and wilfulness is suspected, your case may be passed on to the Criminal Investigation Division.

Now your position changes some. Now you are faced with a possible prison sentence if their charges get past a jury. Your only defense may be an incorrect inventory figure. Remember, now you're under oath. Are you going to *swear* that inventory figure was correct? Did you actually count it yourself? If not, are you sure that whoever did count it recorded it accurately? Even if you did count it, long into the night, couldn't you have been off by as much as your discrepancy? If you waited until mid-January to take inventory, couldn't there have been some purchases that came in after the first of the year which shouldn't have been included in your beginning inventories? Go on, admit you could have made a mistake. Nobody's perfect, right? So you may have to pay more taxes for the previous year; the special agent wasn't concerned with that year when you were charged, so you are not convicted for it. You pay the back taxes and get back on good terms with Uncle Sam, and you do not go to jail—directly or indirectly. And from now on, you'll keep better track of your inventories than ever before.

When your inventory is livestock or crops, the IRS has a whole different row to hoe. Farm inventories—even from small ones operated on the side—can cause a criminal investigation to go astray, especially where livestock is involved, whether it strays or not. Many farmers are not required to maintain inventories by IRS; instead, they base their profits on sales and expenses on a special tax form just for farmers. If an investigation should be launched against one of these men in the field, it can be difficult to determine his net worth at either end of the year, or fluctuations in inventories. Livestock bred during the year by animals bought in tax periods gone by, unsold or ruined crops, can account for increases or decreases in inventory and inflated or deflated net-worth figures at the end of the year. How can they figure your correct income for two or more years ago when there's no way to find out what your beginning inventories were then? This doesn't mean a farmer who doesn't keep inventory records is safe from the IRS, it simply means it will be more difficult for an agent to establish his beginning net worth, especially if he's conducting a criminal investigation.

DEPRECIATION

Much to the dismay of many taxpayers, the current tax laws usually do not allow you to go back and claim depreciation deductions you could have claimed in previous years. If you don't take it in the year you're entitled to it, the deduction may be lost forever—or at least until they change the law. By the time you face a tax auditor, and find out your accountant didn't deduct the maximum amount of depreciation to reduce your tax liability, it may be too late. So you're stuck with it, just because that @&*$% accountant (make that ex-@&*$% accountant) didn't claim all the deductions he could have.

However, if it's a criminal investigator you're facing, it may be time to pounce. Borderline criminal cases have been dropped when it was pointed out that the taxpayer wouldn't owe so much tax had his accountant claimed the maximum depreciation deduction, which could be as much as double the regular straight-line depreciation. Even more if you can add in additional first-year depreciation. Increase depreciation expenses $20,000 for instance, and taxes for that year could be decreased significantly. So significantly, in fact, that the case may lose any jury appeal it might have otherwise possessed. After all, would a jury convict a person who only owed two dollars in additional tax? Technically it might be a crime, but it's not, you know, a *crime*. Anybody could be off by two lousy dollars, for Pete's sake! A jury of your peers is most likely to sympathize with someone who's had as much trouble understanding the tax laws as they have themselves.

Even if you read the IRS publications on the subject, it can still get confusing: "Ordinary depreciation is . . . computed on the cost or other basis of the property, less the additional first-year depreciation deduction and salvage value." So says the 1979 "Tax Guide for Small Business." It says a lot of other things too—*a lot*—and you almost need a guide to the guide to figure out what it all means. So it may be perfectly plausible for you to claim you only figured it out *after* your return had been filed and the investigation commenced. Makes you wonder what other deductions you might be missing.

BAD DEBTS

Something else you could have inadvertently left off your tax return was the deduction for a bad debt. The law says a debt becomes a loss when it is deemed uncollectible. The tricky part comes in when you try to decide *when* it became uncollectible. Lazy Louie promised to repay you that $6,000 he borrowed by July, four years ago. Four years later there is still no sign of the money—or of Louie. You could have deducted that debt as a loss three, maybe four years ago. But you keep thinking, Louie's a good egg at heart, he'll come through—someday.

That six-thousand-dollar deduction could have come in handy last year, you think to yourself as the auditor pores over your tax return. It was a good year, last year was, and your taxes were higher than ever before. "Could I file an amended return and claim that debt as a loss now?" you ask the auditor eight months after filing.

"If you wanted the deduction, you should have thought of it when you filled out your return," the auditor might reply, sounding like a prerecorded message.

"Does that mean no?" you inquire innocently.

"Oh, yes," he replies; and you begin to perk up until he adds, "that means no." (Some may allow it—it depends on the individual situation.)

Well, you'll just have to wait and deduct it next year. Just your luck, that's when Louie will decide to come through; so you won't have a bad debt to deduct anymore. And if you had deducted it last year, and Louie came through this year, you'd only have to report it as income this year—so you're back where you started from.

If your IRS agent is of the "special" variety, it could be to your advantage to bring that bad debt to his attention, since it could throw a wrench into his criminal case. Knowing how difficult it would be to disprove your allegation that you just forgot to deduct it, he's likely to allow it, where the auditor would not.

PAYMENTS ON ASSETS

Now that you are no longer intimidated by tax men, you will have no fear when it comes to revealing the sale, trade, or acquisition of assets— whether business or personal. Now you realize they

221

don't tax the entire selling price you charged for various assets, but only a portion of the profits. For instance, if you sold your tool set for $500 and made a small profit, they could tax the whole selling price unless you reveal the source of that $500. You'll still have to pay some tax, but not nearly as much. It is certainly preferable to pay $10 in tax on that sale than the $150 they might have charged you if you had kept it a secret. You only made a $75 profit on the deal, you quickly point out, and part of that was nontaxable. And how would the agent even find out about the $500 amount?—by your deposits or an indirect method.

Be sure to tell the agent about any trade-ins he might mistake for expenditures. If you did not get back all of your original costs for an item you traded or sold, there may be no profit to tax. This is true whenever simple return of capital is involved. Of course, if you had deducted a depreciation expense for that asset, and you sold it for more than your book value, then you'll probably pay taxes on the difference.

Where the sale of assets is concerned, you should consider not only your original cost, but any additional money you may have spent on improvements, which can also decrease your ultimate profit. For instance, you paid $30,000 for your house when you bought it five years ago. When you sell it for $40,000 it does not necessarily mean you had a $10,000 profit. If you added twenty mimosas and a dandelion patch to the landscape, installed central air conditioning and built-in burglar alarms, all those improvements (as opposed to general upkeep) should be added to your costs. Thus, your actual profit is more like $5,000. (Maybe you should have charged more.)

Maybe you paid one hundred dollars for an old, unfinished table while on your vacation in scenic Secaucus, New Jersey, last year. It looked so nice after you finished fixing it up (the table, not Secaucus), someone offered you two hundred dollars for it, and you sold. But, be careful! Your profit is not one hundred dollars; you have to add to your original cost the cost of the paint, stain, brushes, Spiderman decals, even your transportation back and forth to the hardware store to get these items. The point is, any increase in your cost means more nontaxable return of capital. But don't start going wild and make yourself out to be some kind of flea-market ace, (unless you are, of course); you still have to pay taxes on those profits. Just remember, the more you can add into your cost, the lower profits you'll have to pay taxes on.

PERSONAL LIVING EXPENSES

Here is a category where you should think conservative. Many people seem to think they spend more on themselves and their families than they actually do, and this can easily make it look like you earned more than you did. Even in a Specific Items method, the more you claim for living expenses, the less you can claim for unreported business expenses. To protect yourself from overestimating, it's a good idea to check over your personal expenses carefully before the audit, to make sure they're accurate when it comes time to tell the tax man. Of course, if he did not request such information in your audit notice, don't bother. But if he starts asking these questions during an audit, it may be wise to tell him, "I need to check over my records." Then prepare a list when you have more time to think about it.

Don't forget, an overestimation of just ten percent on your grocery bills can cost you about $90 in additional federal taxes. This applies to people in about a thirty percent tax bracket, like the Humperdinks in Chapter 9, filing jointly, earning $23,000 in taxable income a year, who reported $3,300 for groceries when they actually spent only $3,000. A single taxpayer who overestimated his bills need only make $16,000 in taxable income to get stuck with the same liability. Keep in mind that it's easier to get the auditor to accept a higher estimate if you should revise it later on. After all, it means more taxes for the IRS. Conversely, he might not be so willing to accept a lower estimate, which you probably won't be able to prove.

Remember, too, that the auditor can squeeze you into a corner by inadvertently doubling up on expenditures. If you itemized the interest from an auto loan as a deduction, then he should not count that interest under "Loan Repayments." Only the principal should be listed there; the interest has been entered separately. So don't let him add together the twelve checks you paid on that loan, or your application total could be off by the amount of interest he forgot to deduct. Taxes withheld from a salary you drew is another item that could cause double trouble. They may have been part of your gross wages, but you never got a chance to apply them—they were automatically applied for you. Only if your gross salary is listed as a source should he enter your withheld taxes as an application. But if he just lists your net salary as a source, and then lists those taxes as an application, there will be a discrepancy that shouldn't have been there.

Is it beginning to sound complicated? That seems inevitible when you start talking taxes, but it's not really all that complex. Just remember: Overestimating your personal living expenses can cost you more taxes than you rightfully owe.

Deductible Expenses You Didn't Pay

Anyone who gets a mileage allowance or per diem in the course of his work, like a traveling salesman, can run into trouble when it comes to accounting for excess applications . . . as if he doesn't have enough daily troubles already. The guy who peddles Super Dooper Blower Uppers from town to town may receive, and subsequently deduct, $4,000 for operating his car; but he drives a high-mileage Tyonda that gets fifty-nine miles to the gallon of gas and hardly ever needs oil or servicing. So, what mileage allowance the Blower-Uppers salesman doesn't spend on gas and oil he puts into his bank account, for the time when he finally takes a pit stop. And now an IRS agent is doing an indirect method on him, and is all ready to tax that mileage allowance he used to increase his bank account. Now is the time for the traveling salesman to point out the source of that money. He doesn't have to do much of a selling job to convince the agent that it's all nontaxable. The agent already knows that. So no additional taxes are assessed. The salesman feels so fortunate at this turn of events that he tries to sell the agent one of his Blower Uppers. The agent does not buy.

Other nontaxable funds you should remember are such items as casualty-loss reimbursements and business-expense reimbursements.

The "I-Should-Have-Paid-More-Attention-in-Math-Class" Excuse

It can be embarrassing to be told by a tax auditor that your understated income was the result of a mathematical error on your part. You thought you'd been so careful filling out that tax return, and now he's sitting there telling you what to do with your decimal points. Once you have been apprised of the errors of your ways, you sheepishly admit your arithmetical incompetence and pay the piper.

If a special agent gets in on the act, however, he might get right back out when he discovers how bad your math is. It is when he starts to verify those atrociously added records that he may begin to feel his case slipping away. Yes, you were indeed guilty of understating your income, and, much as you hate to admit it to the Calculating Wonder, you do confess. There goes another criminal case out the window. It had all the necessary elements except the main one—intent. After all, you didn't make those errors on purpose and you didn't realize you'd made all those profits, did you? Maybe you can invest part of them in a math tutor.

CHECKS IN TRANSIT

If you deal on a cash basis—that is, you don't consider sales complete until you've been paid—you have probably developed a lot of patience waiting for tardy checks to arrive so you can balance your books. When it happens during the year, the IRS takes no heed, but if that large check you expected in December doesn't arrive until January, it shouldn't be counted as income on last year's return.

Then there are checks you received in December but didn't deposit until January. There may have been only a few days between receipt and deposit, but in that brief interim, out went the old year and in came the new. Now, do you report that income on last year's return, or this year's? Technically it was available to spend last year, and that's the year it should be reported. Then you count it as cash on hand for the beginning of the new year. Remember, the more cash you had on hand at the beginning of the year, the more nontaxable moneys you had available to make those applications auditors are so fond of listing on their indirect methods.

Even when the method employed is of the direct variety, cash on hand can make a difference. The less you reported you had available at the beginning of the year, the fewer unreported business expenses you'll be able to apply to it, if you happen to think of some later. After all, even if you do remember other business expenses after the fact, the IRS will want to know how you paid for them.

When it comes to year-end receipts, you may have a real problem trying to remember whether that check arrived in December or January. The bank-stamped date could offer a clue; it's something the IRS is very likely to heed. The bank stamps can be off occasionally—sometimes as obvious as "November 32, 1899" or sometimes by just a couple of days. But if the bank stamp says "December 29," they probably won't believe you received the check in January, especially if it is stamped the twenty-ninth in more than one place. However, if it's stamped "January 2," it could have come in that very day, or several days previously—who's to tell? You are, that's who. To an auditor, if it's not reported as income one year, it must be reported the next. You pay taxes on it either way.

But a question arises in a criminal case. If you really cannot remember whether you received that check before the end of the year, or on the date it was stamped, January second of the following year, are you willing to swear it came in at the very end of the very year they're prosecuting you for? Or were you going by that bank date and saving it until this year's tax return was due? If you were intending to pay taxes on that money this year, they can't very well accuse you of *wilful* evasion of taxes on that check with the terrible timing.

You're Nominated

Someone else has asked you to sell his valuable antique moonshine still, promising you a ten percent commission on whatever price you can get for it. Before you can find a buyer, however, your friend hops a plane for parts unknown, leaving you with the still. Congratulations, you have just become a nominee.

With that moonshine still parked conspicuously in your back yard, you feel compelled to sell it as soon as possible, before those nosy folks from the Bureau of Alcohol, Tobacco and Firearms (BATF) of the Treasury Department think you've gone into an illegal business. You find the perfect buyer in the Hillbilly Museum of Not-Very-Modern-but-Not-Ancient History, which writes you a check for $5,000 and promptly takes the still off your hands. You subsequently deposit the check into your bank account to await your friend's return, at which point you'll sign over $4,500 of that to him, keeping the other five hundred as your well-deserved commission. When he finally arrives six months later, looking tanned and mellow, you complete your deal.

Well, you avoided BATF, but then along comes the IRS, an even more potent division of the Treasury Department. Now they want to count that $5,000 check you deposited into your account as unreported taxable income. You point out that you kept only $500 of that money, and as always, they demand proof. A notation on the receipt you happen to have kept, reading "for moonshine still," might suffice, but that doesn't prove you sold it for someone else.

The check for $4,500 you wrote to your friend ought to do it. If you can't prove it (if it had been a cash transaction, for instance), you may feel the hungry hand of Uncle Sam reaching into your pocket. Next time you'll think twice about accepting nominations. In fact, you might not even run.

If someone else should ask you to hold some money as his nominee—even after you point out that banks are doing that sort of thing nowadays—you'll want to be sure you get some kind of documentation of the transaction, just in case the IRS holds *you* responsible for paying taxes on that money. That's what you get for being such a pushover who doesn't keep records.

The preceding checklist contains some of the more common traps that can throw off both direct and indirect methods of proving income. Most apply to all the methods; but some methods have their own problems due to the peculiar way they are structured. The Unit and Volume method, for example, may not accurately reflect income since not all customers may pay the same price for your units, or some shipments could have been rejected. Percentages do not necessarily account for hidden differences between ostensibly similar businesses: After a percentage comparison is done, several of the businesses may expand while one goes out of business, so can the comparison between them stand up? Neither of these methods is used very much, since courts may not even accept them as evidence. But if you are that uncooperative or your records that inadequate, it may be the only recourse available to the IRS.

If you're operating on an accrual basis, your exact

income for a given year may be difficult to pin down. How do you determine precisely when Accounts Payable and Accounts Receivable accrue? Were they posted accurately at the beginning and end of the year? Make sure the IRS employs the same kind of accounting method you do, or your figures may not match. And whenever there's a mismatch, the IRS gets suspicious. At any rate, do not swear to the correctness of your figures unless you are absolutely positive they're right. Better to be wrong and free than sit in jail surrounded by your righteousness.

Sometimes it seems the IRS inhabits a world all its own, completely removed from the rest of us mortals. They have their own private language, their own particular way of gathering information, their own little games that no one else can play. No wonder you may feel a gulf between you and the agent on your case. But remember, it's his job to communicate with you, and if he can't get through to you one way, he must try some other means. It's not all up to you to bridge the gap. So if you don't understand him, say so; make him explain himself clearly. It could affect the outcome of your case. You may not get a lasting friendship out of it, or even a passing acquaintance, but at least you understood the things that count. You may instinctively want to blame him if the figures come up wrong, but don't forget, the fault could easily have been yours, or your accountant's. After all, nobody's perfect.

PART III

Of Interest to the Criminal Investigation Division

If the only function the Internal Revenue Service had to perform was the collection of taxes, it would be a smaller, less awesome agency. However, unless a wave of honesty sweeps over the land tomorrow, our myriad tax laws will remain in effect, continue to be broken, and so necessitate the need for enforcement. Just as your city police force serves to enforce local ordinances, so, too, does the IRS enforce the farther-reaching Internal Revenue Code. And, as the tax laws expand, so does the agency that carries them out.

The vast majority of tax cases never go beyond the Examination or Collection Divisions. And the worst the civil authorities can do to you is add penalties to your tax bill—or refer your case to the Criminal Investigation Division. If one of their special agents is able to prove you wilfully broke a tax law, you could face fines and/or prison sentences, in *addition* to the taxes and penalties assessed by the Examination Division.

Only a very small percentage of taxpayers will ever find themselves in a courtroom facing criminal charges relating to taxes. Of those who are prosecuted, only a small percentage will be acquitted. IRS special agents are trained to drop weak cases and concentrate on those with the best chances for conviction. Then the resulting publicity will serve as a deterrent to others. According to 1979 statistics 3,338 cases were referred for prosecution during 1979, but only 1,820 taxpayers were formally charged that year. Of those charged, 1,270 taxpayers pleaded guilty of nolo contendere (no contest), 342 were convicted after trial, 86 were acquitted, and 183 had their cases nol-prossed or dismissed. These are not very high numbers compared to the millions of taxpayers in America who have yet to capture the IRS's attention.

If you should ever become one of the unfortunate few against whom the IRS decides to launch a criminal investigation, this section may give you some idea of what they're after, and how to defend yourself. Of the major tax crimes that will be covered, both civil and criminal aspects are included so that you may gauge your options accordingly.

Perhaps your tax return will never come near the big, bad Criminal Investigation Division. That does not mean *you* won't—in another role. One day, perhaps when you least expect it, a special agent may walk into your life and begin asking you questions—about *another* taxpayer of your acquaintance. For each case investigated, special agents must contact dozens of witnesses. If ever you are one of these witnesses, your testimony could make or break a case. That's something that is directly of interest to the Criminal Investigation Division.

CHAPTER 16

Affidavit Afterthoughts

Wilhelmina Goodperson was flabbergasted. She had just been summoned to U.S. District Court to testify against her boss in a tax case. How in the world could this have happened? She's always minded her own business, never meant to hurt anyone, did an honest day's work for an honest day's pay, for which she dutifully paid her taxes, or rather, her boss did, through withholding. And now poor old Mr. Underhand was being charged with tax fraud? And Wilhelmina, the faithful employee, would have to testify against him? How could she do that, when good old Mr. Underhand had just given her another juicy raise—just because she was "such a good egg"?

At the U.S. Attorney's office, the IRS agent who was assigned to the case reminded her of a certain affidavit she had signed, which attested to Mr. Underhand's curious method of banking his employees' withholding taxes. Although Wilhelmina swore to the fact that she wrote that check every Friday like clockwork, somehow it never reached Internal Revenue. Now the IRS had collected enough evidence to prosecute Mr. Underhand, and Wilhelmina's signed statement made her a key witness. But it was over a year ago that the tax man had visited her! Wilhelmina had nearly forgotten. Would she really have to say those awful things about dear old Mr. Underhand—and in front of a judge and jury, too? What if her statement was wrong? That tax man sure didn't spend much time verifying it. What was his name? Maybe she hadn't told him all she thought she did. After all, it's been so long, it was hard to remember what she'd said. And now, she was expected to repeat it—in court! Oh, dear, what now?

You may never have any trouble with the Internal Revenue Service yourself, but somewhere along the line you might come across others who will. If they should be investigated, you might find yourself in the role of a witness. If an IRS agent has reason to believe you can shed some light on the case he's investigating, he may call on you to make and sign a statement about the offender, who could be your employer, a relative or neighbor, a business associate or partner—anyone whose financial dealings you might know something about. If it's a criminal investigation, you may even be asked to affirm the suspect's knowledge of tax matters.

Every month hundreds of people are asked by IRS agents to swear or affirm to the correctness of a statement concerning an associate's activities, financial and otherwise. Your affidavit will help to support evidence they may already be gathering against him, and later might refresh your memory if you are called on to testify in court several months or years later. The agent may have outlined the statement in advance, and ask you to complete, sign, and swear to it if you believe it's correct; or he may transcribe the testimony you give him for your signature. That may be the extent of your involvement in the case . . . or it may not.

When you signed the affidavit, you were sure its contents were true. But later you may begin to wonder if parts of it could be misconstrued, or perhaps it just wasn't quite accurate. Could you get into trouble for it? Could you possibly take back what you said, and correct it? What will become of that statement?

To maintain your peace of mind, it's always a good idea to request a copy of the affidavit for your records at the time you make it. If you don't ask for the statement itself, at least jot down the name of the IRS agent who took it from you, the office he works out of, and the date; or ask for his card, on which you can record the date and the party you discussed. Then, if you want to amend your statement, he may be able to locate your affidavit more easily when you phone in your request.

If you want to change or reword your statement, simply contact the agent to whom you originally gave it and let him know of your wish. He or whoever is currently handling the case will be glad to accommodate you. Usually you will have to make a new statement to amend the original one. If you failed to do so the first time, ask for a copy; or at least be sure you *make a record* of what was said, to whom you said it, and the date. You can be very sure that the IRS agent did.

You may never hear anything more about your affidavit, or what became of it. Don't bother asking the agent, because there is usually no way he can be sure. The investigation may be dropped long before the case comes to trial. Even if the case does go to court, your testimony may not be necessary: The defendant could plead guilty or nolo contendere, or his attorney could stipulate as to fact what was contained in your statement, thus saving you a trip to the courthouse.

And if you are asked to testify, you'll be allowed to read over your statement first in case you've forgotten portions of it. The affidavit could also be used to impeach your testimony if it conflicts with your original statement.

Of course, you'll be very careful to tell the truth when you make your statement; but if it is later proved to be false, there is a slight chance you can be convicted of wilfully making a false statement. This misdemeanor is punishable by a fine of up to $1,000 or up to one year imprisonment or both, according to Section 7207 of the IRS Code. The punishment is not handed down often, because very few people are charged with this particular crime—simply because it is so hard to prove. Yes, the affidavit is supposed to be true and correct—but only *to the best of your knowledge at the time you made the statement*. Even if you later admit that your statement was incorrect after all, you may have believed it when you first made it.

You do have one other option when an agent asks you for a statement. You can refuse to talk. But IRS agents are a stubborn lot; if they really need your testimony, they won't take no for an answer. They will slap you with a summons, ordering you to testify. Agents usually have a few prestamped, blank ones handy, for those occasions when they run into particularly reluctant witnesses. They may be reluctant to squeal, but they could be even more reluctant to go through all the legal hassles a summons connotes.

"Greetings," it begins cheerily. "You are hereby summoned and required to appear before_____, an officer of the Internal Revenue Service, to give testimony relating to the tax liability or the collection of the tax liability of the above named person for the period(s) designated, and to bring with you and produce for examination the following books, records and papers at the place and time hereinafter set forth."

Under the Fifth Amendment to the U.S. Constitution, you do have the right to remain silent, if your statement would tend to incriminate you. But, if the IRS believes it would not incriminate you, then you can be charged with failure to comply with a summons under Section 7210 of the IRS Code. It's a misdemeanor carrying a maximum fine of $1,000, one year in prison, or both, together with the costs of prosecution. A high price to pay for keeping your mouth shut—especially when it didn't even concern you personally to begin with.

One would-be witness who had been summoned pleaded the Fifth Amendment in answer to every question put to him, even "Have you given this statement freely and voluntarily?" and "Is there anything further you care to add for the record?"

"I refuse to answer on the grounds that it might tend to incriminate me," he recited—so many times it began to sound like a recording.

It wasn't that he had anything terrible to hide; it

appeared he was just one of those people who refuse to let themselves be bullied or "railroaded" by anyone in authority. When they took him to court, he even refused to let the judge inspect his records in camera (private chambers). For his trouble—which was not even germane to the IRS investigation at that point—he was found in contempt, and the judge sent him to prison, presumably until he decided to talk.

The summons can be a rather persuasive conversation piece, but the taxpayer who is being investigated can fight it, under the law. In its attempt to limit the abuse of summonses, Congress now requires that a taxpayer be notified when a third-party record-keeper, such as his bank, has been issued a summons concerning him. A copy of the summons must be given or mailed to the taxpayer in order that he will have at least fourteen days to contest his record-keeper's compliance. If he does contest it, then the IRS is denied access to the information they had summoned. But then they will probably take the matter to court, where the third party is usually compelled to comply with the summons—unless the taxpayer can come up with a very convincing reason for denying the information to the IRS. If the taxpayer loses the case, he may wind up paying the third party's legal fees.

Whenever the IRS contacts you as a third-party witness, it's a good idea to make a record of the meeting for your permanent files. It need not be elaborate: All you need is the agent's card with a brief notation of what was discussed, and the date the conversation took place. Then, if you should ever want to amend your statement, you can do so easily. You can refuse to answer IRS questions under the Fifth Amendment, but the IRS can answer back with a summons. If you still refuse to answer, they may take you to court, where you will be ordered to testify on the spot unless you can prove the information may incriminate you. Taxpayers who are subjects of IRS investigations may contest summonses of their third-party record-keepers, but the odds favor the IRS. They can be awfully persistent when the testimony is important enough to their cases. On the other hand, your story might do them about as much good as a Mother Goose rhyme, which means your only contact with the IRS was nothing but a waste of time . . . unless you managed to wangle some free tax advice out of the agent while he made his brief appearance in your life. At least he wasn't investigating *you*.

Some witnesses don't even bother to wait until the IRS comes to them for their testimony. They actually make the initial contact themselves, which could open a case the IRS had previously been unaware of. What makes these pigeons so eager to squawk? The next chapter contains a clue.

CHAPTER 17

Informing:
Modern Day Bounty Hunting

Essentially, the United States government relies on the honesty of the majority of its citizens in order to collect the taxes it needs to run the country. Realistically, however, there are enough taxpayers trying to avoid this unpleasant obligation as to keep a monstrous bureaucracy working full time to uncover the cheaters. Over the years the Internal Revenue Service has developed many and varied methods of finding tax dodgers, from simple observation to complicated computer cross-checks, in order to keep pace with the mounting national debt—however improbable a proposition that may be.

One little-publicized method has its origins outside the formidable IRS. Once in a while honest citizens come across other, less-than-honest citizens whom they know or suspect are not paying the government their fair share. The IRS may or may not know about the tax dodger, too, but an alert outside informer could provide them with a valuable lead. If the outside information subsequently leads to the collection of the unpaid taxes and penalties, the informer may receive a percentage of that revenue as his reward. The percentage varies from zero to ten percent, depending on the usefulness of the information.

Perhaps you know of someone who seems to be living beyond his means, or a business acquaintance with two sets of books. Maybe you'd like to get revenge on a person who has cheated you and is probably cheating Uncle Sam, too. It may simply be jealousy that motivates you, or your realization that the less taxes that are collected from others, the higher your taxes will have to go to compensate. Whatever your motives for informing on someone else, you should know how the reward system works, for, if you don't ask for a reward (and many informants don't), none will be offered. The IRS will collect the outstanding taxes and penalties, and you will receive their nonnegotiable thanks—or not even that.

The essential thing to keep in mind when informing is *specifics*. It's not enough merely to give the IRS a person's name and address and inform them that he is cheating on his taxes. In determining whether you deserve a reward and how much it should be, the IRS decision maker (usually the district director or his representative) will ask himself, "Would we have caught this person on our own, without your information? How much did we have to discover ourselves?" He might decide your calling the delinquent to the IRS's attention merits one percent of the taxes and penalties collected, or that you deserve the full ten percent (up to $50,000) for providing documented proof of wrongdoing. The whole reward system is arbitrary, with little statutory basis to go on. Whether or not you receive a reward, and how much you get, depends largely upon the subjective judgment of your district director.

Let us assume that your next-door neighbor is Teddy Taxdodger, and you suspect he's evading his taxes. You do a little covert snooping, maybe ask a few casual questions, and soon you discover how he is able to afford his rather extravagant life-style, while earning about the same amount of money you do: He is cheating the U.S. government. Now that you know there could be some money in it for you, you may consider risking Teddy's wrath by informing the IRS of his transgressions. Your identity will be kept confidential, but he might still figure out who tattled, by a simple process of elimination. Oh, well, you never liked him much anyway.

In particularly delicate cases, or when the IRS solicits more information from you, the chief of Criminal Investigation may assign you a code number, to further protect your identity. "007," maybe. Real cloak-and-dagger stuff.

Once you decide to inform, you should phone or write your nearest IRS office and tell your story. If they think it has possibilities, an agent will follow it up. And if, as a result of your tip, an investigation is launched against Teddy T., you must be sure to fill out IRS Form 211, Application and Voucher for Reward for Original Information. This will legally assure you of receiving your reward, if one should be warranted.

On Form 211 you will list Teddy's name and address, as well as yours and your Social Security number, the name of the IRS agent to whom you furnished the information, and the date. The date establishes the fact that you, rather than an IRS agent or someone else, were the original source of the information.

Several months could elapse between the date you first brought your inside information to the agent's attention and the date you fill out Form 211. By that time you could have forgotten the original date and the name of the agent who received your tip. Now it can be harder to prove that it was indeed you who supplied the information, but it can be done. Chances are the original agent took down your name and address as a matter of course; so verification will already be on file, and your claim for a reward can proceed unimpeded. If for some reason you did not give your name during your initial report, you might still prove your claim by simply repeating your original tip—information which no one else but the original informant would know. But you can save yourself a lot of trouble and aggravation just by making a note of the date you furnished your information, and the name of the agent who received it from you—the same data that will be needed on Form 211.

What kind of information is the special agent interested in? Well, if you merely tell him that Teddy Taxdodger is dodging taxes, he'll ask you for details. Is he neglecting to report all of his income? Is he overstating his expenses to make his profits look smaller? Can you cite specific means he is using to dispose of his unreported income or excess profits? The special agent will be particularly interested if you can point out specific traceable assets Teddy may be trying to conceal, such as real estate, cars, or interest in a business. And if you can tell him how you know all this, your story will sound more credible and action is more likely to be taken.

There are any number of schemes the IRS looks for during an investigation. Put yourself in an agent's place, and see if you can uncover any of the following activities Teddy might be up to:

1) He fails to record a percentage of his daily sales.

2) He seems to be skimming off five or ten percent of all monies taken in before giving receipts to the bookkeeper to add up.

3) He overstates expenses, such as fuel bills, by, say, twenty percent.

4) He owns a number of rental properties, but fails to report the rent he is collecting from them.

5) He claims fourteen dependents when you know he's childless and hardly speaks to his wife.

6) He has a separate business apart from his primary source of income which he fails to mention to the IRS. Anyone who does odd jobs in his spare time, free-lancers, or people who hire themselves out from their homes are good possibilities in this category.

7) He maintains a secret bank or stock account, possibly under an assumed name, where he is hiding some of his income. This one is obviously difficult to find out about, but if you can turn up a lead, you will have supplied some good, solid evidence the IRS might never have discovered on its own. It could happen; some people like to brag, you know. And if you pass the word along to the right people, your chances for a reward increase.

8) He appears to be living beyond his means. He

might have built himself an expensive swimming pool, bought new cars for each of his children, or showered his wife with furs and jewels. Any of that could generate suspicion when you know that Teddy earns no more than the average blue-collar salesman.

The more facts you can furnish, the better chance the IRS will have of catching your tax-dodging neighbor. For instance, if you can tell them approximately how much money you believe he's concealing, so much the better. The larger the understatement, the greater the chances they'll take steps to tax it. And ten percent of that tax money could wind up in your pocket. Then again, the district director may decide to give you only one percent; some people have been lucky to get two percent. Suppose you were fortunate enough to get as much as five percent. Translated into dollar signs, this means you might wind up with about $350 for showing that someone underreported his income by $20,000, which ultimately yielded a total of $7,000 in tax and penalties. Five percent of $7,000 equals $350, even during inflationary times.

Keeping your ear to the wall can produce all sorts of interesting information, provided, of course, that it's the right wall. If you happen to work in a savings or full-service bank—particularly in the trust department—you have a better chance of stumbling across tax-evasion schemes than if you spend your days driving a truck. Employees of brokerage houses, postmen, bookkeepers, secretaries—each may be in a good position to eavesdrop. And if your city or county has a high crime rate, chances are that unreported payoffs are changing hands in the vicinity of City Hall.

That's another avenue you can explore. Once you've enlisted the aid of IRS in cleaning up City Hall, there could even be additional rewards and honors in it for you from grateful fellow citizens. On the other hand, perhaps you would prefer to remain anonymous.

If you do decide to inform to the IRS, be prepared to face a lot of uncertainties. Keep in mind that the Internal Revenue Service is subject to the Privacy Act and various disclosure laws, which will prevent them from revealing details of their investigations to you. You may never know whether your reward was just one percent of the additional taxes, or the full ten percent. If you don't get a reward, what happened? Did the IRS act on your information? Is your credibility in doubt? Were they too busy with other matters? Did the suspect actually report that additional income? All sorts of questions can begin cropping up in your mind as you begin to wonder if you'll ever be rewarded for your amateur sleuthing. And you may never learn the answers.

Remember, not only is your percentage, and the reward itself, not guaranteed, it could be years before you ever collect. If your information is truly useful, the IRS will probably act on it—sooner or later. If it's acted on only by the Examination Division, everything could be settled in two to three months. But, depending on its complexity and how much further digging the IRS agent must do, it could take two years or more before all civil and possible criminal matters are resolved. Also, Teddy could keep the case in litigation for years by appealing to higher courts. So it could be quite some time before Teddy actually pays his taxes and penalties. And only when his payment is finally received can you collect your reward. Remember, it will be based on the actual amount of taxes and penalties *paid,* not the amount assessed. A lower figure may have been agreed to during the interim. By the way, if you move during this period, it might be wise to notify your former district director of the new address to which he may send your reward. Remind him what it's for, and when you supplied the information, or else your letter might not make any sense to him.

That reward money could come in handy. You might already have plans for it. Is there any way you can find out when you can get your hands on it? Even an approximate date would help, if you're planning to pay for your vacation with it. If you just call the agent and ask about the progress being made on the case, he probably won't tell you, because he knows he can be sued for disclosure of confidential information. But if you inform him that you have uncovered additional information pertinent to the case, and he is anxious enough to hear it, he might at least let slip the fact that an investigation is in progress. He might even drop a hint as to how much longer it could take, in light of your new lead. Having learned what *you* wanted to know, you then keep your part of the bargain, and tell him your latest tidbit. He may already know about it by now, but at least you have learned that "your" case has not been "misplaced" or filed away in some forgotten internal cranny. On the other hand, you could find out just that: They are *not* following up your lead, in which case you might as well forget the reward money. It would have been taxable anyway.

To qualify for the ten percent reward—or part of it—remember you have to fill out IRS Form 211. The more useful leads you can supply about your suspect, the better your chances of instigating IRS action on the case. It may be a long time before you hear any more about it, so be sure to keep a record of your tip, the date, and who took the tip from you. The reward system is arbitrary, and none will be paid until your suspect actually pays his taxes and penalties. You may be able to get a few hints out of the IRS agent by tempting him with new information you've uncovered, but like your reward, it's not guaranteed.

If you must make contact with the IRS, it's better to be a witness than a suspect. You now know what precautions witnesses should take, but what if you find yourself in that other unwanted role? Just what sorts of crimes might they suspect you *of*? And what are your options when the testimony that interests them concerns *you*? The following chapters address themselves to these questions.

CHAPTER 18

So You Failed to File a Tax Return

He lives in a state of anxiety, bordering on dread. Each day he nervously checks the mailbox, hoping against hope the feared letter isn't there. The jangle of the telephone sets his nerves on end, and strangers take on the sinister appearance of spies, all out to get him, all unmistakably aware of his guilt. Relief comes only when he retires each night without having his secret discovered; but sleep is fitful—for tomorrow, the apprehension begins all over again.

These symptoms appear in late April, and grow progressively worse with each passing month. Some clever victims are able to conquer successfully the condition by convincing themselves that they have gotten away with their little deception, and no one will ever find out. But the guilt that accompanies failure to file a federal income tax return can strike any American taxpayer—or rather, nontaxpayer. If you did not file your return when you should have, it could happen to you.

Your anxiety arises from the fear of what will happen next. With so many millions of tax returns to process, the IRS could easily overlook the fact that yours is not among them. But what if they do find out? Will they come after you with guns and warrants, slap you with outrageous fines, throw you into prison with killers and thieves, tar your feathers? Will they be more lenient if you muster your courage and humbly confess to your sins?

By the time you reach the end of this chapter, your worries may be over. Or at least—considerably diminished.

Most people are at least vaguely aware that there are laws against failure to file a federal income-tax return. How serious a crime is it, and what are the penalties? The Internal Revenue Code considers it a misdemeanor, punishable by a maximum fine of $10,000, up to one year in prison, or both. That's the criminal side of it. Civil penalties are also assessed on the amount of additional taxes owed, beginning from the date they were due. A delinquency penalty of five percent per month can accumulate up to five months, for a maximum total of twenty-five percent. In addition, the IRS assesses a penalty of .5% (1/2 percent) per month for failure to pay on time, also beginning from the date taxes were due. These two civil penalties can add up to a maximum of 47 1/2 percent over and above what you would have paid the government had you filed a return and paid your taxes on time. And if they tack on the five percent negligence penalty, you could wind up paying a maximum 52 1/2 percent in nondeductible civil penalties. Add to that the tax-deductible interest that will have accumulated, and you face a hefty bill. (And if you were subject to the estimated tax penalty, your bill will be even higher.) Remember, civil penalties apply to the tax owed, not to the interest on it, which is a separate charge.

If you are found guilty of civil fraud in connection with failure to file, you could pay a maximum fifty percent penalty, in which case the failure-to-file, failure-to-pay and negligence penalties would be nullified. For example, if you owed $3,000 in taxes on April 15, 1979, and failed to file a return, you could end up paying the IRS a total of $4,680 if the government caught you exactly one year later. That is, the original $3,000 tax, plus $1,500 for civil fraud, plus $180 in interest, figured at just six percent per year. So, failing to file and pay that tax cost you an additional fifty-six percent, of which only six percent can be deducted from next year's taxes. And that's just for civil purposes. Criminal conviction could have cost you another $10,000 in fines, raising your financial burden to $14,680—not counting legal fees. And don't forget the possible prison sentence. All for that $3,000 tax. No wonder the tax dodger feels troubled.

But perhaps he had a good reason for not filing. He might have been seriously ill, or maybe he had been held hostage ("Of course I would have filed, but I was tied up at the time"), or he just didn't have enough money left to pay Uncle Sam when April fifteenth rolled around, or . . . there could be any number of reasons. The IRS will take related circumstances into consideration in each individual case, before recommending penalties. While the thought of all those penalties may strike terror into your pocketbook, there are ways you can make things easier on yourself.

First, it may be of some comfort to learn that no criminal investigation is likely to be launched against someone whose tax liability is less than $1,000, and the chances of it happening to those who owe nothing, whether they file or not, are almost nil. Generally, special agents only concern themselves with taxpayers who fail to file at least two years in a row because it shows a pattern of wilfulness. The Criminal Investigation Division does not like to spend thousands of dollars and man-hours on a case they can't use as an example for the rest of us.

That's not to say you're entirely safe from detection. The IRS's central computer can be programed to match this year's returns with those filed the previous year and automatically send letters to taxpayers on last year's roster for whom no return can be found this year. Sometimes the IRS letter is all that is necessary to persuade the reluctant taxpayer to ante up. And of course, the sooner he pays, the less interest and/or penalties will have accumulated.

But some people have a way of "forgetting" to answer their mail. Deep within the bowels of the Collection Division, a revenue officer may take this non-response as an open invitation to a personal visit—not to be confused with an audit. When a revenue officer comes to call on someone he suspects did not file a tax return, he's there to learn three main things:

1) Have you filed a return this year?
2) If not, why haven't you?
3) Do you plan to file, and if so, when?

He will also request that you file your return through him, if and when you decide to do so, in order to keep track of the case. Unless he is remiss in his duties, he will be very careful *not* to solicit a return, because this could hamper any criminal investigation that may follow. In fact, if he does solicit a return, and you are subsequently criminally investigated for failure to file, the criminal part of your case can be dismissed for that reason alone.

Although it's possible to escape detection by the computer, IRS has still other ways of catching up with delinquents. Among the various methods that have been employed are active searches of selected professions—such as lawyers, doctors, accountants, and other self-employed people in a good position to hide income, and tips provided by state tax collectors or individuals.

Perhaps it's been so long since that year you failed to file, you're positive the IRS has long since forgotten about it. Surely the statute of limitations has run out by now? If you have read Chapter 3, you may recall that the statue varies from crime to crime, and that in civil cases, there is no statute of limitations for any year you were required to file and did not. They're not likely to pursue the matter if little or no tax was owed, but the fact is, if an IRS agent should discover you didn't file a return in, say, 1956, you can still be held liable for any taxes due for that year, plus interest and penalties. (Actually, they seldom go back more than six or seven years unless adequate records are available.) For criminal failure to file, the statute of limitations is only six years; remember?

Your concerns, however, may be more immediate.

Here you are on a collision course with April fifteenth, not knowing where you're going to get the money you owe the government. One legal way out of your dilemma is to request an extension period by filling out IRS Form 4868, which will automatically give you an additional sixty days in which to file your return. Of course, interest and the failure-to-pay penalty will still be applicable after April fifteenth. Depending on your circumstances, IRS may grant you still another filing extension of up to six months after the initial grace period runs out. In this case you must state your reasons for your request on another form—2688. Your request will be honored if you have a good enough excuse, such as your records were destroyed in a fire, or your bookkeeper used your canceled checks for confetti. It will normally *not* be honored for what is usually the actual reason: 1) you don't have the money, or 2) you'd rather spend it on something else. So it may help to be "creative" when filling out this form; not dishonest, mind you, just i-m-a-g-i-n-a-t-i-v-e. Remember, these extensions apply only to filing your return, not payment of taxes.

Another prospective gambit: Go ahead and file on time, but without including your payment. Though not strictly legal, this at least will protect you from those heavier failure-to-file charges. One half percent per month (for civil failure to pay) is easier to handle than the five percent per month (twenty-five percent maximum) you would have had to remit for failure to file a return.

Wilful failure to pay is another matter. In *Spies* v. *U.S.*, the Supreme Court stated, "We would expect wilfulness in such a case to include some element of evil motive and want of justification in view of all the financial circumstances of the taxpayer." In another case, *U.S.* v. *Palermo*, the high court said that repeated failure to pay taxes coupled with large expenditures for luxuries when taxes were owing may be wilful.

So, if you continually spend all your money on riotous living and leave Uncle Sam off your list of recipients, the IRS may have grounds for charging you with criminal failure to pay under Section 7203 of the Internal Revenue Code. If you are found guilty, you could be fined up to $10,000, imprisoned up to one year, or both, and have to pay court costs as well.

Before they proceed with prosecutions, however, the IRS does try to learn the reasons taxpayers failed to file their returns. As they identify the hardship cases, deaths, taxpayers who have moved, Johnny-come-latelies, and honest misers, they are left with a handful of holdouts who have refused to cooperate. Some of these cases will be turned over to the Criminal Investigation Division. If you are one of these unfortunate few, a special agent will be dispatched to your domain, and the focus of the investigation changes. Now the primary goal of the IRS is not to get you to file and pay your taxes (although you're still liable, of course), but to convict you of a crime. You will have been chosen as an "example," and your case will be publicized as a deterrent to others. If it does finally get to court, you have a good chance of being convicted. A special agent makes every effort to insure that there are no holes in his evidence, and that the case against you is as airtight as possible. He will be interested in where you have been living, any progress that has been made on your return since your last contact with the revenue officer, and who was responsible for filing your return. Of course, the ultimate responsibility lies with the taxpayer, but sometimes you may be the victim of an unscrupulous accountant, or assumed your spouse filed a joint return for you. Ultimately, the special agent hopes to prove three things:

1) You did not file a federal tax return.
2) You should have filed.
3) You knew of your requirement to file.

As far as the last item is concerned, ignorance can be an asset. Section 7203 of the Tax Code specifically cites *wilful* failure to file on the part of the taxpayer—that is, you deliberately intended not to file a return when it was due. If you tell the special agent that you didn't know you had to file *every year,* for instance, he may have a hard time proving otherwise. And if he can't prove you knew of your requirement to file, he has no case.

Of course, even if you don't admit you knew of your requirement, there are several ways to prove item three. The most obvious evidence rests in your previous returns, tucked securely into the files of the IRS. If someone else used to prepare your return, that person could fulfill the knowledge requirement. Business associates, friends, relatives, customers, your lawyer—anyone who has dealt with you—may likewise be questioned by the special agent during his investigation of you. He may even go back to your college transcript—no matter how long ago you attended—to see if you took any courses relating to tax matters. All of your financial dealings are subject to his scrutiny. Thus your bank records, ledgers, net worth, and spending habits could all be examined, whether or not you answer the special agent's questions. The special agent's investigation could take three days, it could take two years; the length of time until your arraignment is equally as varied. By the time the special agent has collected all the facts and figures pertinent to your case and sent his report through legal channels, you could well find yourself in U.S. District Court answering charges of failure to file a tax return or returns, of failure to pay taxes, or perhaps both. The back taxes, interest, civil penalties, and fines you face could be enormous. A prison sentence is a possibility, also.

There is a simple way to avoid such an ordeal. It will almost certainly cost you some money, but not as much as if you wait for them to come to you. If you know you're guilty and don't wish your whole life turned topsy-turvy by the IRS, it may be prudent for you to go to them. Confess your transgressions, file your return, and pay up. You could still be criminally charged with failure to file on time, but the chances are extremely remote. The vast majority of IRS agents would be hard pressed to recall any cases of taxpayers being prosecuted after making a voluntary disclosure. So, coming forward of your own accord could well prevent you from being branded a criminal, although you may still be liable for civil penalties.

But suppose you have evaded your taxes for so long and owe so much that you can't possibly come up with enough money to meet your liability? Here is a situation that will be dictated by individual circumstances. Excuses abound, ranging from being victimized by Pasquale's Pizza Parlor & Collection Agency (sounds reasonable) to squeezing all the material pleasure out of life your income could allow, with no thought of paying taxes (a not-so-good excuse; in fact, it's terrible). If your particular circumstances lean toward the former helpless predicament, the IRS collectors are more likely to understand when they finally receive your tardy returns, and ask when you plan to pay them ("Of course I would have paid on time, but it was a choice between paying Pasquale or paying a surgeon for fixing my broken bones"). But if they find out you were playing the Prodigal Son with a vengeance when some of that money should have gone to Uncle Sam, they're sure to take a dim view of your actions. Here's where a good tax attorney may provide a guiding light. Even if you confess—now that your fortune has run out—they could still prosecute you for wilful failure to pay. Of course, they realize your attorney would call attention to the fact that you came forward on your own to file, and that your conviction could discourage others from making voluntary disclosures, so they may just decide to treat it as a civil matter—again, depending on your circumstances.

Once you've admitted to the IRS how much you owe in back taxes, they will naturally want to collect them. A letter containing their bill will usually arrive first; but if you don't answer it promptly, be prepared for a visit from a revenue officer. It is his function to collect outstanding taxes any way he can. He may seize property—business or personal—sell possessions, attach bank accounts, etc. On the other hand, he could set up a collection schedule, allowing you to pay in increments over a period of time. This last option can occur if, in the revenue officer's learned opinion, you are making an honest effort to pay the tax, and the IRS would have little to gain by seizing all your assets.

How do you convince a revenue officer of your sincerity? You could try turning on the tears as you relate a pitiful tale of woe, but chances are all you'll get out of the tax man is a tissue (they often carry boxes of paper hankies for just such contingencies). You'll usually get more sympathy if you stick with cold, hard facts and down-to-earth predictions. As with auditors and revenue agents, figures mean more to revenue officers than bleeding hearts. You could start by showing him a net-worth statement, (with properly depreciated assets) and all those burdensome *liabilities* that prevented you from paying your taxes on time. But the tax collector is more interested in how you plan to pay Uncle Sam; so you also produce a profit-and-loss statement which illustrates in numerical order how your business is improving, your liabilities gradually being reduced, and your outlook brightening. (Salaried workers might use chronological statements from creditors that show a steadily decreasing balance.) Using these documents as your firm foundation, project that mounting prosperity into the future to demonstrate your potential ability to pay your back taxes—maybe not all at once, but little by little. Point out that, despite conditions in the marketplace, demand for your product or service will remain high, or even rise. For instance, if you sell firewood, you could predict a big jump in sales as other fuel prices burn holes in people's budgets. If the agent has been threatening to seize your saws, point out that you will then be deprived of a means to pay back those taxes. By allowing you to keep your business going, he'll not only get his money, but you'll be earning even more income for them to tax and staying off the welfare rolls. By the time you've presented your well-thought-out arguments, you might have gained an ally from the IRS. As has happened in the past, maybe he'll drop by your place every so often around bill-paying time, and collect whatever you're able to pay. Once in a while business may be off and you won't have anything for him, except maybe a good joke to brighten his dreary day. But the next week you proudly hand over a check for $250; $75 the week after that; and so on, until your taxes have finally been paid. That's about the best sort of relationship you can have with a revenue officer, if ever you have to deal with one. It's all in how you present yourself to him. Let him see you as a responsible citizen who really will come through when the hard times are over, and he's likely to help ease your burden.

If, after listening to your tales of woe, the tax collector decides there is no possible way you will ever be able to meet your tax liability, the district director is authorized to accept offers in compromise—that is, they reduce your tax bill to the maximum amount they think you can pay; and after you pay it, they wipe your slate clean. That's what happened to some moonshiners when the "Revenooers" finally caught up with them in their hillside hideouts. They had kept no records, but they sure as heck didn't have as much money as the IRS claimed they owed—a ridiculously high figure, based on what sales could be traced, projected over a year. So, some of these moonshiners were allowed to pay a fraction of the liability computed for them, and the IRS let it go at that. (Who knows, maybe the tax men got treated to a strong dose of "hillbilly hospitality" as part of the bargain! Gives you a nice, warm, "generous" feelin'.)

What if your conscience gets the better of you just when the government has caught you? If you decide to file a return after a criminal investigation has already been instigated, this may help the government to prove intent. It could suggest that you know of your requirement to file. However, the sooner you pay your taxes, the lower your total bill will be, because interest and penalties will no longer be accumulating. This step should also be taken if you decide you have right on your side and want to sue the government for a refund. For more details about suing the IRS, see Chapter 5.

So you failed to file a tax return, or you're contemplating doing so? Now, at least, you know your options. You can hope Uncle Sam doesn't detect your offense, take a chance on being investigated by a special agent—and possibly convicted; or come forward voluntarily and confess via a late return. Of course, if you can't pay, you may get a visit from a revenue officer.

A large portion of the revenue officer's decision will be influenced by his perception of your ability to pay your taxes at the time they were originally due. You may have had the money then, but chose to spend it on a twin-engine executive jet instead. He's not likely to be very sympathetic in cases like that. He'll probably sell the plane for you and keep the profits for the IRS, if you have enough equity in it. If the thought of losing your plane, yacht, rec room, or Chevy makes you want to pack them all up and fly as far from the IRS as you can go, stop! There may be other ways out of your dilemma. A competent tax lawyer may have some good ideas if you're unsure what to do next or if you think your rights are being violated. Generally, though, it's better to file late than not at all.

CHAPTER 19

A Few Minor Alterations

You've struggled and sweated and burned several thousand gallons of midnight oil to reach your present respectable income. Congratulations! You've just earned yourself a higher tax bracket. As if you weren't paying enough taxes already, now that you've gotten your promotion, Uncle Sam wants more! That leaves you with about forty-three cents more than your after-tax income before the promotion. It's enough to make you want to cheat. Oh, nothing major, like claiming thirty-five dependents, or simply refusing to pay taxes. Well, no, you're too honest for that. But just a few little, bitty, teensy, tiny changes here and there—an extra zero on a charity contribution here, a forged letter from a finance company there—now you're back down to the amount you were just starting to grow comfortable with. You've paid the same taxes you always paid, kept that extra income you worked so hard for—and no one is any wiser . . .

Oh, no? Well, try to slip those altered documents past a trained Internal Revenue Service auditor, and you might be in for a rude awakening. And once your eyes have been opened, another unpleasant experience could be in store: not only an assessment for additional taxes and interest, but a civil fraud penalty of fifty percent of the additional taxes, and a court penalty of up to $10,000 or five years in prison, or both. That's if you are charged with submitting altered documents under Section 1001 of the U.S. Code, Title 18. But if you're convicted under Section 7207 of the Internal Revenue Code, it's only a misdemeanor instead of a felony and your maximum punishment (besides that fifty percent civil fraud penalty) is a mere $1,000 fine, one year in prison, or both. So if you ever face a fraudulent document charge, at least hope they apply the Internal Revenue Code, rather than Title 18. On the other hand, better not to give them the choice in the first place.

You don't spend two, four, six, or eighteen years in the Internal Revenue Service without learning some tricks of the trade. Having completed a rigorous training program and a dozen or so audits, an IRS agent grows more and more familiar with the Games Taxpayers Play to wriggle out of their tax bite. He learns to look beyond the typical nervousness to the true deception lurking beneath, and his ability to detect altered or false documents has become almost instinctive.

Of course, you may never get audited, so your secrets will remain safe. And even if a tax auditor does start snooping around your books, you may still be able to pull a fast one on him—especially if he's inexperienced, half blind, and has an upset stomach; or if you are a master forger and an accomplished actor. This last is a paramount requirement for carrying off your little charade; for while you're watching the auditor thumb expertly through your most intimate financial affairs, you'll no doubt be seething inside, particularly when he comes to those retouched checks and checkered receipts. That's when you'll have to look as confident as a poker dealer with a stacked deck.

He knows you're nervous. They usually are; it's expected. Maybe he'll try to calm you down a bit with a little small talk; "Nice weather we've been having," he might say, or, "This coffee is delicious, can I have another cup?" or, "I just love poisoning pigeons in the park, don't you?" So you relax, feeling lucky you got such a nice guy for an auditor . . . but maybe he's not so nice after all. Maybe he has a reason for wanting you relaxed and unsuspecting. Somewhere along the line he may ask casually, "Did you change banks this year?" or "Is that figure right?"

"Yeh, that's right," you answer, now that you've been lulled into a somewhat secure state; then you continue babbling about your pet cockatoo that he seems so intrigued by. Anything to take his mind off your accounts. But that is exactly where his mind always is. After all, it may be an inconvenience to you, but to him, it's his job. And while you're chewing your fingernails to the nubs, or pretending disinterest, or showing off your mathematical skills, the auditor is putting on a performance of his own. He is comparing what you say (about your records, not your mother-in-law's lumbago) to the documents before him. And for anything that doesn't match up, he makes a note.

If you look closely, you might notice a slight

change in his facial expression when something looks fishy to him. Oh-oh, is it that six-dollar check to the "Save the Knock-kneed Kiwi Foundation" which you changed to sixty dollars? But you were so careful to leave just enough space between the original six and the two little zeros to fill in another zero where the decimal point would have normally gone (so 6 00 became 60.00). And of course, it was an easy matter to add a "ty" to the original "six." You used the same color ink exactly, too; so how could he tell?

Elementary, my dear taxpayer. He simply looked in the lower right-hand corner of the check, where the bank stamps the amount your check cleared for. This "bank-encoded" amount is imprinted onto every check so their computer can read it; but any fool can, too, and the auditor is no exception. He is trained to look for bank imprints, which he can easily compare with the amount written on the check. So, if your check reads "Sixty_____ and no/100_____ Dollars" and the bank code is stamped "0000000600," he knows the check only cleared the bank for six dollars, and you are most certainly trying to deceive him.

Sneaky, isn't he? And auditors have lots of other tricks up their sleeves, too. They also look for out-of-sequence checks, or one check that's a different color or texture from all the rest—any such inconsistency arouses suspicion. You could have a perfectly good explanation for this seeming anachronism, and the auditor is perfectly willing to listen to it. He may even believe you.

You might also find yourself caught in a lie while trying to prove the truth. Perhaps you'll be asked to document a deduction you took for medical expenses, but for some reason you've lost or misplaced your canceled check to Dr. Coldfinger. You know very well you paid the guy $852 to add your kidney stones to his collection, but there is no record of it. So you dig out canceled checks from previous years, find one made out to Dr. Coldfinger for $175 (the shyster!) and another for $592; update them to the present year with a few deft strokes of your pen, and voilà—there's your proof.

If you're really clever, you'll also change the dates the bank stamped on the check, usually in more than one place, so that they all correspond. That's something else the auditor will be looking for. But even if you alter all the dates on the check, your scheme could still backfire—if they decide to audit last year's return as well. Now you've already used up the documentation for that year's medical expenses, explaining this year's—and you're stuck.

There are some telltale signs of alterations even an amateur can spot—because they were so obviously the work of an amateur. Misspelled words, typographical errors, erasures (or worse, cross-outs), absence of letterheads on "official" documents—all cry out for recognition; they all say "somebody's been tampering with me; guess who?" Come, now. Did you really think an IRS auditor would let a "&" pass as a "$"? All right, maybe it *was* an honest mistake on your creditor's part, but every other document you produce from him shows he knows the difference between dollars and ands. If there's anything worse than a document faker, it's a careless document faker. It practically guarantees at least an assessment for additional tax, and perhaps a visit from a special agent, too.

By the time a special agent shows up, he has studied and digested the auditor's report which lists his suspicions of your altered documents. During his interrogation you tenaciously stick to your original story, knowing the agent is looking for items of intent through conflicting statements. He will take special notice of the documents in question, and may contact the appropriate third parties to verify or disprove their contents—your bank, payees, whoever made out those questionable receipts, and so forth. When the bank, for instance, verifies their stamped amounts in the lower right-hand corners, your guilt will begin to solidify in the special agent's mind.

The special agent will want explanations, and, as they say in those grade-B Hollywood adventures, "they better be good." "Where is your canceled check to Seabiscuit's Glue Emporium that you want to include as a business expense?"

"Oh, I paid them in cash," you toss off.

"But for every other Seabiscuit's invoice, you have a canceled check to match," says the agent, fingering the one invoice with a different typeface and absence of code words. Are you sure you want to stick to your glue story?

Later the agent asks, "You say you make $12,000 a year—yet you contributed $3,000 to your church??"

"I'm a loyal disciple. I gladly pay the twenty-five percent tithe."

"And what about this payment to Fred's Fat Farm for $444? There is no other record of your doing business with them," says the agent.

"Of course not, it was a one-shot deal; I-I wasn't happy with their service; that $444 went right down the drain."

The special agent gives you a look that makes you feel about two inches tall, rechecks the auditor's report, then makes a notation in his handy notepad. He'll go on grilling you until he is either satisfied with your story or with the auditor's inclination to disallow this deduction. It's safe to say he is probably inclined toward the latter. He knows you've lied about the contribution to the "Knock-kneed Kiwi Foundation," so why not Fred's Fat Farm?

You'll make his job a lot easier if you would just confess—preferably in writing—to altering those documents, so the tired, overworked IRS agent could just go home to dinner and leave you in peace. One trick some agents like to employ to speed the process along is bringing your family into the picture: "Did your wife fill in this figure?" he might ask, or, "So your daughter erased this word?" He's counting on you to rush to the defense of those you hold dear, protecting them from any taint of guilt, at which point you could blurt out your confession. Of course, if you're on the verge of a bitter divorce and your daughter has been nothing but trouble since the day she was born, you might be quite willing to let either of them take the blame. But then, the special agent probably checked out your domestic situation before trying this particular gambit.

Sometimes another party really is to blame. There have been cases where an innocent taxpayer has submitted documents to the IRS, not knowing they had been altered by someone else. If ever there was a good time to pass the blame, this is it—because, after all, this taxpayer didn't alter the documents, the other guy did.

The Internal Revenue Service is just as alert for written lies as they are for oral ones. Expertly altered documents may go undetected, but IRS agents are experts, too, and can often catch little discrepancies that the ordinary Joe would miss. The more obvious alterations are good for a laugh, especially when they come in multiples. One not-so-wise guy tried to slip no fewer than ten forgeries past the IRS. All had been Xeroxed, for uniformity, and to cover up the places that had been changed on each document. The trouble was, in two cases, the little square of paper that had been laid over the letter stood out in stark white contrast to the otherwise gray sheet, and the edges of the smaller paper could be easily discerned. This amateur forger even wrote receipts to himself on blank pieces of paper, simply filling in the amount and signing the name of the payee himself. He had also typed a letter to himself under a finance company's letterhead, boosting his interest deduction considerably. Although he was obviously guilty of submitting false documents, his case never reached court because of the relatively paltry amount owed. But he still had the civil fraud penalty to contend with.

If enough evidence can be found, and a large enough amount of unpaid taxes, the special agent will recommend the taxpayer be charged with wilfully submitting false documents. The current policy of the IRS will determine whether the defendant will be tried under the Internal Revenue Code Section

7207, or the more specific—and harsher—Title 18. Compare them yourself:

U.S.C. Title 18, Section 1001	IRC Section 7207
"Whoever, in any matter within the jurisdiction of any department or agency of the United States, knowingly and wilfully falsifies, conceals or covers up by any false, fictitious fraudulent statements or representations, or makes or uses any false writing or document knowing the same to contain any false, fictitious or fraudulent statement or entry, shall be fined not more than $10,000 or imprisoned not more than five years, or both."	"Any person who wilfully delivers or discloses to the Secretary any list, return, account, statement, or other document, known by him to be fraudulent or to be false as to any material matter, shall be fined not more than $1,000, or imprisoned not more than one year, or both."

Which one will they choose if they prosecute you for this crime? "Eenie, meenie, minie, moe . . . No telling which way the policy will go."

In gathering evidence, the IRS will have looked for: check amounts that don't match the bank imprints on them; altered dates; out-of-sequence checks; checks of differing colors or textures; unordinary or excessively large payments to a particular party; typographical errors, erasures, misspellings, and cross-outs; absence of letterheads; Xerox copies that are not uniform; missing checks or invoices; and your own testimony to the auditor and special agent. If your explanations check out, you will retain your innocence. If not—well, you always wanted your picture in the newspapers, didn't you?

If there's anything the IRS disapproves of more than false financial records, it's a plain old fabricated tax return. To find out how they react to such things, see the next chapter.

CHAPTER 20

Who's Responsible for This?

At the bottom of your tax return form there is a prepared declaration awaiting your signature. If it sounds threatening, it's supposed to:

> Under penalties of perjury, I declare that I have examined this return, including accompanying schedules and statements, and to the best of my knowledge and belief, it is true, correct, and complete. Declaration of preparer (other than taxpayer) is based on all information of which preparer has any knowledge.

Section 7206 (1) of the Internal Revenue Code is more specific. Here the threat sounds even more sinister:

> Any person who wilfully makes and subscribes any return, statement, or other document, which contains or is verified by a written declaration that it was made under the penalties of perjury, and which he does not believe to be true and correct as to every material matter . . . shall be guilty of a felony and, upon conviction thereof, shall be fined not more than $5,000, or imprisoned not more than three years, or both, together with the costs of prosecution.

And that $5,000 fine and three-year prison sentence can be pronounced even if someone else prepared your tax return. The IRS knows that many taxpayers who wish to go the fabricated-return route rush to a preparer so they can later try to pass the blame.

It doesn't matter to the IRS whether you supplied your preparer with every single financial record you had during the year; if they catch a discrepancy or false information on your return, they will come after *you*, not your preparer, at least for the current tax. And returns filled in by tax preparers are just as subject to examination as those completed by the taxpayer alone. So it is up to *you* to check over the return for any omissions, inaccuracies, or misstatements. Once having satisfied yourself that everything is in order, you can sign with a clear conscience, and face any audits that may follow with the same confidence.

Professional tax preparers can be very helpful, especially when your finances are somewhat complicated, but they can't read your mind. Some of the things you should be prepared to discuss with your preparer are:

1) Your method of accounting

2) Additional income besides your regular earnings

3) Business assets you may have purchased or sold during the year, along with amounts paid or received

4) The method by which you ascertained the value of your inventories

5) Questionable deductions and expenses; some things that you thought were deductible may not be, or vice versa

You might get a few more ideas of what to tell your preparer by skimming Publications 17, "Your Federal Income Tax," and 334, "Tax Guide for Small Business." (If nothing else, they can help cure insomnia).

You may have thought that having someone else prepare your tax return would not only save you time and trouble *before* April fifteenth, but later on, if you should be called for an audit. Then you could let the preparer worry about all the details, and answer all those tedious questions . . . and explain any errors he might have made. A convenient way to pass the blame, right?

Wrong! Although the preparer may participate in the audit and answer questions about how your return was prepared, it is still your return that's being questioned, and you must bear the ultimate responsibility for the correct tax.

If the auditor says, "You overstated your expenses by $11,000. You owe an additional $4,000 in taxes," beware of pointing the finger at your accountant. He could point right back and claim, "He failed to supply me with correct information; he said nothing about that $11,000 business expense being for his sister's plastic surgery. When I asked for details, he said it was for remodeling his store."

"Well, it was," you pipe up. "My sister was a clerk last year—and that plastic surgery certainly improved the looks of the store."

But now that the auditor has uncovered the truth, get ready to write a check to Uncle Sam. Not only have you tried to deceive the auditor, but your accountant as well. The latter cannot be held responsible for false claims on your return, when it was you who failed to supply the correct information. Your wilfulness in this case will advertise itself like a neon billboard. Don't be surprised if you're assessed an extra $2,000 for civil fraud, in addition to the $4,000 tax plus interest. Something this fraudulent could also prompt an investigation by a special agent (see Chapter 21).

Another example: When your accountant pleads innocence while you assert he failed to include additional income, which is the auditor to believe? When it comes down to a matter of your word against the return preparer's, either one could be telling the truth; but you are the one who had a financial gain by not paying the taxes.

So the auditor will probably ask you why you did not check your return to make sure that income was included, and he'll want to see the records you claimed you supplied to the accountant. Maybe you tell the auditor you have used this accountant's services for years without problems, and you don't bother to check his work; but you still produce the records in question, which satisfy the auditor as to your honesty. Now he may indeed begin to suspect your accountant did not include all of your income. This does not let you completely off the hook—you will still owe additional tax and interest—but the accountant may be the one charged with preparing that false return. The civil penalty for this is $500; and if he is criminally prosecuted for wilfully aiding or assisting in the preparation of fraudulent returns, whether or not authorized, he can be fined up to $5,000, imprisoned up to three years, or both, plus cost of prosecution. And if it can be proved a tax preparer falsified one return, it follows he would not be above doing the same with others. In that case the IRS may examine other returns he prepared. If these, too, are fraudulent, the preparer may be subject to that many more counts of the same charge. But if the clients are also implicated in the deception—that is, if they knew what the preparer was up to, and went along with it—the charge could be conspiracy to defraud the U.S. government, a felony carrying a fine of up to $10,000, ten years in prison, or both.

Laws and regulations like these are making preparers think twice before filing other people's tax returns. Most are well aware of the penalties they face, and will try to acquire all the information necessary to prepare a "true, correct, and complete" return. In this way they protect themselves from subsequent accusations by clients eager to pass the blame. Of course, not all preparers will take the time to make a thorough study of your financial data; some may simply ask a few cursory questions—like, "Are you sure this represents all your income?"—and are willing to accept your every "I'm sure" and "That's correct" without further question. The preparer has no reason to doubt your word—but an IRS agent might, later on. So tell your accountant the truth, even if he doesn't ask.

That's what Freddie Mindbender should have done. But Freddie kept putting off his taxes, and by the time he arrived at the local office of I. Figger & U. Shlock, all he wanted to do was get it over with so he could make his arm-wrestling league on time. On Friday, April thirteenth, fifteen minutes before closing time, Freddie showed up at I.F. & U.S. with a hastily gathered handful of miscellaneous receipts and canceled checks that he'd thrown into his bureau drawer whenever he happened to think of it. As Darlene Sweatsox, the preparer, patiently proceeded to unravel Freddie's jumbled finances, Freddie kept glancing at his watch and flexing his biceps, as if his tax return was the last thing on his mind. (It was.)

Darlene persisted. "Do you have any proof to back up these expenses?" she asked.

"Sure, sure, they're around somewhere," Freddie said, fidgeting.

"Can I see them, please?"

"Don't worry about it, I'm sure that's the right total, I added it up twice."

Darlene was skeptical, so to satisfy her—and speed things up a bit—Freddie fumbled in his pocket for a scrap of paper, anything that might look like documentation. He came up with his shopping list. Brazzeire for Becky, it read. "Community Chest $68.75," Freddie read aloud. Aspirin, said the list. "Medical expenses, $433.95," Freddie reported. On down the list he went, until all his "expenses" were accounted for.

By the time he reached the end of his fictitious report, he was feeling quite proud of himself. He actually began to believe his own story, and he was sure he had Darlene hooked, too. Assuring her he could back up all his claims, he left confidently, thinking he could always blame Darlene Sweatsox of I. Figger & U. Schlock, if anything went wrong. He finally deposited the return into an official U.S. mailbox at 11:58 P.M., April fifteenth. Naturally, it was postmarked the sixteenth, but that's not what caught the IRS's attention.

Freddie's tax return turned out to be so inconsistent with national averages for income versus deductions that he was selected for an audit. After they met with Freddie, the IRS decided to contact Darlene Sweatsox, who had returned to being a belly dancer at The Oasis nightspot. Darlene explained to the agent, between gyrations, that she had prepared Freddie's return to the best of her ability, using the information he had supplied. Yes, she had asked him for documentation, but she'd never seen it. She'd asked about other sources of income, too, but he'd sworn he had none. It didn't take the agent long to learn that Freddie really hadn't tried very hard to provide the necessary data, for there was much he had failed to tell Darlene about—like his part-time bartending job, and his winnings in the State Arm-wrestling Championships.

Each time the agent questioned Freddie, his answers were different. First he claimed five dependents, and later, two. He never gave the same totals of expenses twice. And always he tried to blame Darlene for messing up his return. But the taxman already had Darlene's sworn affidavit describing her involvement in Freddie's case, which, together with Freddie's inconsistent statements, hidden income, and unkempt records were enough to charge him with filing a false return. Freddie went to jail; Darlene went on belly-dancing, after taking time out to testify against Freddie, who is trying to organize a prison arm-wrestling team.

There are cases in which the tax preparer *will* have

to share the blame for fraudulent returns. Although the majority are honest (at least where their clients' accounts are concerned), there are a few unscrupulous preparers who prey on naive or unsuspecting taxpayers, as well as the U.S. Government. Some dishonest preparers may understate your tax liability, in order to build a reputation as "the guy who saves you tax dollars." Other unsavory characters plan to pocket the money you give them to remit to IRS, which in turn will grow very perturbed when they miss your usual timely tax payment.

Watch out when your new accountant asks you to make your check payable to him, claiming he deposits it into a special account along with his other clients' tax payments, and then mails in a single check covering all of them. The money he collects—earmarked for IRS—may never be remitted. Naturally the "accountant" does not report this ill-gotten loot on his own return, but when the IRS catches up with him—most likely through one of his clients being investigated for nonpayment—that secret account may be subject to taxation and penalties. And by the time he pays the government, he'll have little if any money left to pay all the angry clients who are no doubt suing him, in order to recover the money the government is demanding of them—now past due. Meanwhile the IRS ends up with more than it would have originally received had the accountant sent in the money, as he should have. Not only will they collect the clients' taxes, but taxes on the accountant's account that were supposed to be paid as taxes!

Moral: Always insist on making your tax check payable to the United States Internal Revenue Service. The initials IRS won't do, either. Some people have been known to open bank accounts under names like Irene R. Smith, or I. R. Strange, so that they can divert a little tax money their way.

Like millions of salaried employees, you may have your taxes withheld from your paychecks by your employer, according to the dependents you claimed on your W-4 form. Normally these withholding taxes are reported quarterly, accompanied by Form 941. The top half of this form goes to the Social Security Office for Federal Insurance Compensation Act accounting. On the FICA half are your name and those of your coworkers, opposite the amount of gross salary each was paid subject to Social Security deductions. The IRS is left with totals: total gross salaries, total FICA, and total withholding taxes. Presently they cannot tell from their half of the 941 how much was withheld from whom, although this will change when a new computer program is put into operation. They can still check your W-2 against your employer's copy if discrepancies are suspected.

What can prompt such suspicion? Indications of evasion on the part of a certain business: another case of someone possibly trying to intercept tax money . . . in this case, an employer who illegally holds onto withholdings, instead of sending it to the government. It may escape notice if the evasion amounts to a relatively small sum from just a few paychecks. But if it happens on a broad scale, the underpayment could become more apparent, and an investigation commenced. It happens more often than you might think. According to the commissioner's report, "Nonpayment of taxes withheld from wages is the most serious delinquency problem facing the IRS."

Meanwhile you are fully confident that your taxes are being properly paid—after all, you get the W-2 forms to prove it. But suppose your W-2 is being tampered with? Some employers take advantage of their employees' trust by jacking up the total salaries on each W-2 by, say, $300 each, in order to make their deductible business expenses look higher. If you have retained your paycheck stubs, of course you could detect this hanky-panky. But if you haven't retained your paycheck stubs, you could assume your W-2 is correct, and wind up reporting more income to the IRS than you actually earned—leaving the boss with a few extra bucks, compliments of the unsuspecting staff. Of course, even if a few employees do catch the "error," he can always blame it on the bookkeeper.

The other type of dishonest employer is less subtle. He's the one who lets his employees think the money he is deducting from their salaries is going to the federal government, when in fact he's keeping it for himself. If your employer is one of those who are withholding withholdings, then your taxes are not reaching the Internal Revenue Service. One way employers have accomplished this is by falsifying or just not filing Form 941.

Will the IRS come after you if they don't receive the taxes your employer was supposed to be paying for you? You can't very well accept the blame for something over which you have no control (although it could affect your Social Security benefits, if they find your account has not been paid up). Employees of people who failed to remit withholdings can usually just file their returns as if the withholdings have been paid. Later on, when the business is examined more closely and the discrepancy finally caught, officers from the Collection Division will start dunning the errant employer. Under Subtitle C of the Internal Revenue Code, employers are required to pay withholding taxes, so it is the employer who will face the collection process—including sale or seizure of his inventories if he refuses to cooperate. It makes no difference if the offender is a small businessman or large corporation: If the IRS discovers an outstanding debt, they will come to collect it.

Under the present computer systems the Internal Revenue Service cannot tell you whether they have received your personal withholding taxes. But one way to assure yourself that they are reaching their rightful destination is by checking with your local Social Security office. That's right, Social Security. Remember, they retain the half of Form 941 containing your name and gross salary (subject to FICA). Merely ask the nice folks at Social Security for a printout of your account showing wages reported last year. When they deliver it, at least you know your salary subject to FICA is being reported—to IRS as well as Social Security. In that case chances are your taxes are also being properly paid. And if the printout holds any unpleasant surprises, you might report this bit of information to the IRS—confidentially, if you like. If it turns out your boss has been evading taxes, you could also try for a reward (see Chapter 17).

On the other side of the coin is the employer who is paying withholding taxes each quarter. If you fit this category, it's extremely important that you get your employees to sign those W-4 forms. Otherwise the IRS may later hold you responsible for your employees' taxes at a higher rate: Instead of the married guy claiming six children as dependents, he will look to the IRS like a single taxpayer with no additional exemptions. (Even if your employees don't expect to owe any federal taxes, you could still be liable for what you could have withheld if the IRS catches up with you later on.) A signed W-4 protects you from such an eventuality. It proves why you didn't withhold the taxes and makes the employee liable for any he may owe.

One unfortunate employer learned this lesson the hard way. After hiring about seven seasonal employees, he calculated they would not earn enough to meet federal tax requirements once their exemptions were subtracted. So he withheld only state and Social Security taxes from their wages. When the IRS later asked him why he did not withhold federal taxes, he couldn't prove it—because he had no W-4 forms listing the employees' exemptions. The IRS promptly relegated these long-departed workers to single-taxpayer status, and demanded that the employer pay the taxes he should have withheld, with only one exemption per employee. As it turned out, they later caught up with some of those employees, who had subsequently filed tax returns, and who proved they did have the exemptions claimed. As for those who who could not be traced, the employer was stuck with the tax bill . . . just because he had no W-4 forms on them.

* * *

No matter who stands between you and the tax collectors, you retain responsibility for paying your own taxes. If discrepancies or deficiencies turn up, it's up to you to explain them. Sometimes a dishonest preparer or employer must share the blame, but the burden of proof is still on your shoulders. Isn't that comforting? As if you don't have enough burdens already!

CHAPTER 21

What's So Special About Special Agents?

Not long after the Bureau of Internal Revenue began collecting taxes, during the second decade of this century, it became apparent that certain cost-conscious Americans were trying to avoid their patriotic duty. To insure that U.S. citizens were indeed paying the correct amounts to Uncle Sam, the Bureau brought forth legions of auditors to examine and adjust tax returns.

As the Internal Revenue Code grew, it became necessary to expand the agency that enforces it. There were some laws the examiners were just not trained to handle. Wilful evasion of taxes, failure to file a return, submitting false documents, filing false returns—these were crimes, requiring several months of careful investigation to prove. A crack force of specially trained agents was needed to enforce the criminal portions of the Internal Revenue Code. These agents would be as well versed in law-enforcement procedures as they were in accounting. They would be empowered to go where auditors feared to tread; they would have the right to inspect otherwise private materials, summon witnesses to testify, travel anywhere their investigation led them, and recommend prosecution. And, since they would be law-enforcement officers, they could be called on for occasional bodyguard duty, like providing protection for other IRS employees who were threatened by irate taxpayers.

For a long time they were known collectively as the Intelligence Division. But when the "experts" got through examining the workings of the Internal Revenue Service, as it was now called, the name was changed to Criminal Investigation Division, since that is what they do. The approximately 2,500 officers in this division are called special agents, but they answer to criminal investigators, too. Their function, however, remains unchanged. You may not feel very special when a special agent comes to call, but he plans to concentrate on you much more closely than his counterparts in the Examination Division. While an examining officer may process hundreds of taxpayers during a year, the special agent is probably focusing his attention on no more than three or four. That means that a goodly number of tax criminals are escaping the thorough, but limited, scrutiny of the Criminal Investigation Division. Some tax evaders have also managed to evade detection by simply moving away, leaving no forwarding address and never filing tax returns again. To the IRS it's as if they'd died—the only sure way *you* can get out of the tax bite. But if a special agent wants you badly enough, he'll go out of his way to find you. He might ask your former neighbor what magazines you subscribed to, and get your new address from *Town-skippers' Monthly* or *Gypsy's Home Journal*. Or perhaps he'll trace you through a canceled driver's license or your car's transferred titles.

Special agents don't always "get their man," but it's for lack of trying.

If a special agent ever does subject you to his high-powered microscope, it would be to your advantage to understand what he's doing and what he hopes to accomplish. If you know you're guilty of breaking whatever tax law he suspects you of breaking, you'll have a fairly good idea of what he's after, and perhaps you'll try to stall him off as long as possible. But he may not come right out and tell you exactly what he's looking for; he's not going to reveal much more than he has to. He will identify himself and allow as how one of his jobs is to investigate for "possible violations of Internal Revenue laws and related offenses." From then on all the information gathered will pertain to you. You'll be bombarded with lots of intimate questions about your life and financial affairs, and you'll probably be wondering how your answers might affect his criminal investigation. And, how will the investigation affect *you?*

You also might want to know how he latched onto you in the first place. With so many tax cheaters out there—most of them richer than you'll ever be—why did he have to pick on you? Actually the special agent does not really just pick his victims—er, suspects—all by himself, although he may have some say in the matter. Cases are assigned to him by his group manager based on referrals from the Examination or Collection Division where irregularities are often spotted first, tips from informants, or sometimes because of the agent's own observations of suspicious characters. Also, other law-enforcement agencies may provide leads about suspected tax violators. There are times, too, that an IRS office may single out a specific group or profession—say, lawyers—to see if any of its members have failed to file tax returns lately. Any of these "community leaders" who is subsequently brought to trial will be publicized accordingly, in the hopes of discouraging others from following in his tainted footsteps. In fact, any IRS criminal conviction is held up as public example of what could happen to others, demonstrating that those tax laws really are being enforced.

Perhaps you never paid much attention to those tax stories, except when someone famous, like a former vice-president, was involved. But it's not only celebrities who get into trouble with the IRS—as you found out when the special agent turned his spotlight on you. From the way he's phrasing his questions, he already seems to know a lot about you, too. Maybe you *are* famous, after all.

Since the special agent's job is to gather all the pertinent information about you that he can, he wants to be armed when it comes time to meet you face to face. Once your case was assigned to him, he studied the IRS files on you—not only tax returns, but attachments, notes, revenue agent's reports—whatever was available. He may also have searched public records for anything connected to you. Sometimes he'll call on your lawyer or return preparer, but usually he saves those visits until after he meets with you. If the case was referred by an examiner, he sought out that agent to discuss the case with him. The more he knows about you before the interview, the better questions he is prepared to ask.

During this pre-interview period he is also going to try to determine whether the case even warrants his time. His investigation may take three months to complete, much longer if it's complicated. After he turns in his report, another year could pass before the case passes through a maze of legal channels on its way to the grand jury. Of course, the special agent cannot detect every possible leak that could sink his case, but he'll try his best to uncover any obvious ones. As he scans your files and questions the examiner who worked on your case, he looks for such factors as these:

1) Intent: Was it a mistake or did you do it on purpose?

2) Tax liability: Is the amount high enough to bother with? You can be prosecuted without owing any taxes, but chances of this occurring are slim.

3) Period: How many years are involved? They usually don't accept one-year cases, nor do they care for split years (1975 and 1977, but not 1976). Criminal investigators prefer cases that cover at least two years in a row, since consecutive years of criminal actions indicate a consistent pattern of intent.

4) Does the evidence show guilt *beyond a reasonable doubt?* Is it solid proof, or so-so circumstantial?

5) Is there a good probability of conviction?

6) Age, physical and mental health: Juries may sympathize with invalids, no matter how guilty they are.

7) Education: Some defendants have been acquitted on the basis of unfinished education or a low IQ, pleading they were unable to understand tax laws.

8) Personal and business background: Your reputation may be a factor.

9) Family circumstances: another possible sympathy getter.

10) Taxpayer's attitude: Is it open and cooperative, or are you obviously trying to hide something?

11) Disclosures by taxpayer: If you had contacted the IRS about this matter before they contacted you, this could cause the case against you to be dropped.

12) Requests for extension: Did you get permission to file late?

13) Venue: Do you live in the same district in which you filed?

14) Prior tax history, audit, and collection: These could provide clues as to your propensity to cheat on your taxes, and your knowledge of tax matters.

15) Statute of limitations: Will the usual six-year limit expire by the time your case reaches court?

16) Availability of books and records and third-party testimony: If the special agent can't get to enough of them, he may not get his proof.

17) Responsibility of bookkeepers and other counsel: Maybe it was their fault.

18) Ability to pay then: Were you bankrupt on April fifteenth that year?

19) Financial position now: Has your net worth increased or decreased?

20) Disposition of funds: Can he trace your expenditures?

21) Prior conviction on same facts: In general, if you were convicted of embezzlement of funds, then trying you for evading taxes on those same funds might border on double jeopardy.

22) Admissible documentary evidence or stand-up witness or both: These are necessary for the charges to stand up.

23) Jury appeal: The special agent may be sure beyond a reasonable doubt that you're guilty, but will a jury believe it? He'll ask himself that question throughout the investigation. If the answer should come up negative, the case might be dropped.

He may not detect any factors that would tend to impede the case at first, but something may come to light later on as the investigation proceeds. It could be one of the twenty-three criteria listed above, or something else he was not previously aware of. Since his job is to get convictions, and since he must spend so much time and effort on each case, the special agent will endeavor to make his case as strong as possible. That it was referred to him in the first place may be an indication of guilt, at least in the view of the referring officer. It is then up to the special agent to investigate his fellow agent's suspicions.

Your testimony could go far toward attaining that proof, and he's going to try to get as much as he can out of you on the first contact, while you are still relatively uninformed and more likely to blurt out admissions. He may even pop into your life without giving you advance warning, the better to catch you off-guard. Whereas the special agent is well prepared for his meeting with you, you may have no idea what direction he plans to go, nor what you should say in your own defense. You might begin to feel like the blind man being led to a cliff's edge by his worst enemy. Maybe you felt perfectly safe and secure, until this sinister-looking character and his witness walked into your life and flipped out his badge.

Some special agents seem quite friendly at first; they're from the school that believes "you can catch more flies with honey than with vinegar." But whether they come on like a tiger or a pussycat, they're all after the same thing: criminal prosecution. Of course, even suspected criminals have rights, such as the Fifth Amendment right to remain silent. This and others will be duly recited to you.

"Do you understand these rights?" he asks.

If you don't he'll explain them in simpler terms. Then he'll ask you to waive your right to remain silent and answer his questions. He'll advise you of your right to have an attorney's assistance, but they will not appoint one for you, since you have not been arrested or charged—yet. Once he gets all these preliminaries through your head, the interview begins, provided, of course, that you waive your right to remain silent and don't wish to call an attorney.

The questions seem easy, at first.

What's your name, any aliases you use, birth date and place, parents, addresses during the years under investigation, marital status, children, other dependents . . .

Even during these mundane questions something of interest may come up. Once you've told him that your wife and two kids are your only dependents, he'll wonder why you claimed six dependents on your tax return. Already he has a contradictory statement from you. And that constitutes a large part of his interrogation. Innocent-sounding individual answers may take on an entirely different aspect when compared with 1) your tax returns; 2) other answers you yourself give; 3) your books and records; or 4) the testimony of third parties. Your answers will be taken not only at face value, but in comparison with other statements relevant to your case. The more contradictions, the stronger the case against you will be. That's one reason many experts advise people who are subjects of a criminal investigation to call an attorney before answering any questions or submitting any records.

When the interrogation gets down to the nitty-gritty, what aspects of your finances will the special agent be most interested in? It depends on the individual case, of course; generally he'll want to know something about each of the following, but he'll stay flexible enough to follow up any additional matters you may bring up which were not on his prepared list.

1) CASH ON HAND—at the beginning and end of each year being investigated. The agent knows you could explain excess expenditures by claiming that you had accumulated funds from prior years. Therefore it's very important to him to pin this figure down as accurately and quickly as possible. Then you can't claim later that you used a large nontaxable cash hoard to pay unreported business expenses or all those personal expenses or to buy additional assets. This has been explained in Chapter 15.

2) HOW YOU ACCOUNTED FOR YOUR INCOME—and when you received it. Were you on a cash or accrual basis? Did you go by your sales tickets or bank de-

posits to determine your income? He'll pay particular attention to your December and January figures, since a few days' error here could affect your tax return for either year. For instance, you reported all your deposits for 1977 as income. But some of those checks you deposited in January were actually received in December, and should have been reported on the previous year's return. However, if you were consistent in such a practice, it would be very difficult to prove wilful tax evasion on this one point; you just didn't know any better, that's all. So you thank the agent for calling your mistake to your attention, promise to keep better track of income in the future, and that's the end of that issue.

3) VENUE: If your case does come to trial, they need to know which district to try you in. If you've lived and filed returns in the same city all your life, there's no problem. But what if you've moved since filing the returns in question? Was the return prepared in another district? In which IRS office were your returns received? In which district do the majority of the witnesses reside? Any of these factors can affect venue. Although it is not the usual case, you may wind up being tried in a city halfway across the country, where you've never even been before. (If you have not filed, he still needs to know where you lived when you were *supposed* to have filed returns.)

4) RESPONSIBILITY: Although you're the one who is responsible for *paying* your own taxes, someone else may be to blame for filling out your tax return incorrectly. This is very important because in a criminal

case you can't be held accountable for actions beyond your control. The fault may be your spouse's. The IRS recognizes that some wives automatically sign their joint returns without questioning their husbands who had it prepared, trusting him to have everything in order. In such cases they assume the wife to be an "innocent spouse," devoid of wilful intent to defraud, and concentrate any criminal investigation upon the husband. The "innocent spouse" rule, incidentally, knows no sexual bounds; sometimes it is the husband who sits guiltlessly aside while his greedy wife pleads her case. And sometimes both of them can be held responsible.

The fault could be with your return preparer. Maybe you trusted him so implicitly that you didn't bother to check his figures when he presented the return for your signature.

There are many technical items on a tax return which you may not fully understand. That's why you may have hired a preparer in the first place—he's *paid* to understand them. But when he went down the list of your totals like a driver in the last lap of Indy, you may have become even more confused, though you didn't let on. After all, you also hired the preparer to save time, which you did by quickly taking his word for the correctness of your return, scribbling your signature, and getting it over with. But don't be in such a hurry to hide your ignorance when the special agent starts questioning you about your conversation with your preparer. After having you identify the tax returns he'll present for your inspection, he will ask who prepared your returns, what instructions you gave, who kept your records, and whether you were satisfied your returns were accurate when you signed them. You may not wish to look irresponsible in front of an IRS agent, but if you were out of touch with your finances to such an extent that you really didn't realize your taxes were miscalculated, say so. Of course, your statements will be compared with the testimony of your return preparer or whoever else you may have implicated; but if it checks out, the case against you could be dropped, and the special agent might focus his attention on your preparer. Remember, they don't have much of a case if they can't prove you knew you were doing something wrong. (If the investigation is for failure to file, he'll want to know if someone was supposed to file for you, and if so, who. Who kept up with your income and expenses, and what instructions did you give them?)

If your lawyer had anything to do with your tax return, rest assured the IRS will contact him sometime during the investigation. But if you think you're protected by the attorney-client privilege, think again. Your tax return and its preparation are not considered privileged communication between you and your lawyer where the IRS is concerned, indeed, they were the intended recipient. So, anything connected to the return—the hows, whys, and wherefores as well as the return itself—must be divulged by your attorney. The same goes for accountants. The only circumstance under which your lawyer can refuse to answer IRS questions is if his replies would tend to incriminate *him*. It's the same Fifth Amendment right you were offered. On the other hand, if his answers will only incriminate you, the client, your lawyer has to give them or tell a court his reasons for refusing. He loses more clients that way.

5) INTENT, or wilfulness: This is a hard item to prove, but the IRS has no criminal case without it. Few suspects are going to come right out and admit they cheated the U.S. government on purpose, but the special agent is ever alert for admissions to that effect. "Did you report all of your income during those years?" he might ask.

Not wishing to admit to a crime, you answer after the slightest hesitation, "Uh, yes, sure . . . I did."

"Oh, then you knew to report all of your income?" the agent goes on, trying not to sound too eager.

"Yes," you say again, confidently, not thinking much of it. The agent does, though; not only have you testified to your knowledge of tax matters, but you have admitted your wilfulness when the agent proves you did not report all the income you knew you should have. In his report it will read something like this: "This taxpayer said he knew to report all income, while during those years he understated his income by $_____."

Later, when he asks where you deposit your earnings, you name a nearby bank where your checking and savings accounts are located. "Do you have accounts anywhere else?" he asks.

You reply in the negative, and hope he doesn't find out about those upstate banks where you keep that little nest egg no one knows about, under fictitious names. But suppose in this case he does find out about them, and thus snares a load of taxable loot as well as—that's right, another item of intent. Here you can clearly see how your testimony during the initial (and subsequent) interviews can be turned against you.

6) INVENTORIES: Are the inventory figures shown on your return correct? If not, this could explain discrepancies. Once again you may be inclined to answer in the affirmative rather than admit you—or whoever counted your inventories—may have made a mistake. Whatever you answer, the special agent is more than likely planning to check your inventory records against your return and your testimony, and will ask you to supply any additional records you may have.

7) ASSETS: Whatever business or personal assets you already owned at the beginning of the years under investigation will be figured into your beginning net worth. And items you bought during that period to increase your net worth will show what you did with any unreported income. This will help to show you didn't spend it for additional business expenses. The special agent will want to know what assets you bought, when, from whom, how much you paid, and in what manner you paid for them.

8) STATUTORY GROSS INCOME pertaining to failure-to-file cases. The figure that falls somewhere between your total gross income and net taxable income determines whether you were required to file a return in a given year. If you earned anything below the minimum amount established by statute (it changes from time to time), no taxes will be due. Statutory gross income is figured by subtracting your cost of goods

sold, nontaxable funds (including loan proceeds), and excludable sick pay from your total gross income. Don't subtract business expenses, except cost of goods sold, in determining statutory gross income. Also, don't subtract dividend exclusions, nontaxable portions of long-term capital gains, itemized deductions, or personal exemptions. (Of course, when you fill out your tax return, you'll deduct business expenses, capital-gains deductions, and personal exemptions—whatever deductions you're allowed.) If the agent discovers you didn't file a return because your statutory gross income was below the minimum requirement, he'll realize immediately that there is no case. Even if your statutory gross income is high enough, there may not be enough tax liability to bother . . . well, on to the next target.

9) EXPENDITURES: Juries, it seems, love to hear how other people spend the money that should have gone to Uncle Sam. The more you spent, the more interesting the trial will be, because the prosecution will usually make a big production out of your wild, extravagant spending habits. How dare you indulge in a gold-plated hot tub when children in Appalachia are starving? Besides, a complete accounting of your expenditures helps to show how much money you had coming in, some of which they suspect you did not report on your tax return. It also proves that additional income didn't go for unreported business expenses. You may have a hard time remembering the exact amount of purchases that took place up to six years in the past; but the special agent, in his persistence, will try to get you to estimate at least a minimum

amount. "At least four hundred dollars?" he prompts.

"Oh, no, much less than that," you assure him. You still don't remember exactly how much, so he suggests another figure.

"At least one hundred dollars?"

"Oh, yes, at least that much," you reply, hoping he doesn't think you're a sucker for paying that much for a candle snuffer. When he adds this figure to the long list he has accumulated, an obvious question arises: "With all those expenditures," the agent asks cagily, "didn't you realize you must have had more profits?" Now, do you incriminate yourself or pretend ignorance?

As he explores your canceled checks and other evidence of expenditures, he'll try to get you to classify as many as possible under personal living expenses and net-worth increases. This will be very helpful to him later on, as he starts collecting evidence of unreported income. Having already pinned down all of your nondeductible expenses through your own admissions, he has prevented you from claiming you used that unreported money for additional deductible expenses. And just to make sure those records remain available for as long as he needs them, he'll have them copied or microfilmed as soon as he gets back to his headquarters. Now he's got himself covered if you should get the not-so-bright idea of altering or destroying those documents after he returns them to you.

By the time he reaches the bottom of your list of expenditures, a lot of time may have elapsed, and you may begin to wonder if this ordeal will ever end. It's true, special agents must be much more meticulous and precise in their calculations than tax auditors since it is they who must prove their charges against you. So, where the auditor might have gone perfunctorily down the list in less than ten minutes, accepting your every figure without batting an eye, the special agent will be much more careful to collect evidence which he can verify before a court. And of course, he has his witness on hand (usually someone from the IRS's Examination Division), to make sure you don't try to alter your testimony later on, when you find out how it's being used against you.

10) NONTAXABLE INCOME: Even if you didn't file a return, you probably want to tell the special agent about all the nontaxable items you can: inheritances, gifts, loans, etc. Still, there may have been some you overlooked, and the special agent will be particularly interested in all nontaxable sources, to make sure they are not erroneously added into your understatement. Usually he'll make use of your own admission that you had no nontaxable monies. If you borrowed any money, or were in the process of paying it back, whether to an institution or individual, he'll want to know all the details: Who loaned it to you, was it cash or check, what was it for, how did you repay it? Oh, is there no end to the special agent's curiosity? Are you kidding? He's only just begun!

11) BOOKS AND RECORDS: All through the interview, as the special agent tallies up the guilt which you tried so desperately to refute, he'll be asking you to back up some of your answers with written records. He'll devour your canceled checks, receipts, ledgers,

and notes even more hungrily than an auditor, comparing their figures with your statements and checking for any signs of forgery or other falsification. The more documents you can produce to support your testimony, the better you'll look. However, if further investigation shows some of them to be false, you will have fallen a few rungs in the special agent's eyes. Some of your misplaced or destroyed documents could have come in handy, too, but how were you to know they'd ever be needed again? Well, with or without your help, the special agent will try to reconstruct your financial history from whatever pertinent records he can uncover, and he'll appreciate any leads you can give him.

By the way, now is the best time to supply those leads, especially to deductible expenses for which you have no documentation. Even if you weren't sure they were deductible at the time you filled out your return, bring them to the special agent's attention. Normally the special agent will allow the expenses if he can't prove you didn't have them. Don't wait until your case gets to court to reveal this information, because the judge may not allow new leads to undocumented expenses once the trial has begun. During his investigation the special agent will contact third parties who may be able to shed light on your case: business associates, friends, relatives, customers, accountants, bankers, your foster father on your ex-wife's side . . . Even if you don't supply any leads, he'll probably find most of them on his own anyway.

One defense you might offer the investigator is the capital loss carry-back you reported on this year's return, which reduced your tax liability for the past three years. But the special agent won't be very interested in that, since you couldn't have anticipated the loss when you understated your income two and three years ago. He *will* be listening intently for any offhand remarks you make that tend to heighten your guilt, such as, "Gee, I must have lived off depreciation." To a special agent, it means, "This guy knows at least a little about tax matters. I can use this as an item of intent in my report."

After what seems like several days of extra-malicious torture, the special agent finally packs his briefcase and disappears into the sunset, leaving you a whimpering mass of wilted weeds. As your mind slowly begins functioning again, it will attempt to analyze just what has happened to you. One thing you're pretty certain of: Your life is about to change, and probably *not* for the better. Having reconstructed, somewhat shakily, your interview with the special agent, you may begin to form an idea of the reasons he chose to visit you. You know special agents conduct criminal investigations, so does that make you a criminal? But he hasn't charged you with anything yet. No, you're not a criminal, you're just a suspect. What are you suspected *of*? If you couldn't tell from the interview, contact the agent and find out. Be as persistent with him as he was with you, until you're satisfied with his answer. Chances are he already had a specific crime in mind when he questioned you.

Among the most frequently prosecuted criminal violations are the following sections of the Internal Revenue Code (Title 26 of U.S. Code):

* * *

SECTION 7201: Wilful evasion of taxes, a felony. Maximum punishment: $10,000, five years in prison, cost of prosecution.

SECTION 7203: Wilful failure to file a tax return, supply information, or pay tax. A misdemeanor punishable by $10,000 fine, one year imprisonment, and cost of prosecution.

SECTION 7206 (1): Wilfully filing a false return, a felony. Punishment: $5,000, three years, cost of prosecution.

SECTION 7206 (2): Wilfully aiding or assisting in filing false returns. Felony. Same punishment as 7206 (1).

SECTION 7207: Wilfully submitting false documents, a misdemeanor punishable by $1,000 fine and one year in prison. The same crime is a felony under Title 18 of the U.S. Code (Section 1001).

SECTION 7215: Failure to collect, account for, and pay over withholding taxes. A misdemeanor. Maximum punishment: $5,000 fine, one year in prison, cost of prosecution.

Do any of these sound like something you could be charged with? If not, there are several others they could cite instead; among them, attempts to interfere with administration of Internal Revenue laws, forcible rescue of seized property, assaulting an IRS employee, or failure to comply with a summons.

The summons comes in handy when special agents run into the occasional uncooperative witness who refuses to answer questions. It's the IRS's not-so-polite way of getting people to open up, or else. The official-looking greeting is often enough to get the witness into the IRS office where he can make his statement. If he doesn't show up, though, they might haul him before a judge, who will compel him to answer in open court, unless he can show cause why his testimony would incriminate him. (See Chapter 16).

The special agent hopes he doesn't have to go through all that bother when it comes to tracking down the witnesses in your case. And you can be sure he will track them down. These people will either corroborate or refute your testimony or figures, and may eventually be called to testify at your trial. He'll almost certainly visit your bank to verify your statements, and possibly uncover additional evidence you might have withheld. When specific deposits or withdrawals are important to his case, he or an aide may spend hours searching microfilmed files in the hopes of finding the relevant names.

Even if a key witness has moved away, the special agent is not above traveling whatever distance it takes to secure his testimony. He is supplied with a handful of blank travel vouchers for just such contingencies. Whether he needs to interview a critical witness in Seattle or keep a traveling suspect under surveillance, all he need do is fill out the voucher with flight and destination desired, and he gets where he's going at the taxpayers' expense.

By the time he has contacted the first few witnesses, you may begin to get that uneasy feeling that you're not as popular as you used to be. The guy who was so willing to lend you money won't even give you the time of day now, and your credit cards are not being renewed anymore. Word is getting around: You're the subject of a criminal investigation by the IRS. You may be innocent, but they're not taking any chances. It's not necessarily the special agent who's spreading the rumors, either. He may have kept a low profile and concentrated on the witnesses' statements, without revealing his total objectives. When pressed, he might simply have said, "At this time, I'm trying to verify a tax return," or "verify income." Of course, a lot of people know the difference between special agents and auditors: when a special agent is involved, that's usually serious. He may have his civil side—that is, to ascertain correct liability—but he's also looking for possible criminal violations. And who wants to be associated with a possible criminal? Even if your case is later dropped, it may take you a long time to recover your barely blemished reputation.

At about the time your best friend stops talking to you, the special agent has finally begun organizing all those hundreds of pages of evidence he has collected into a written report, which will be the basis of any criminal indictments that may follow. He could have gotten out of the case any time he found evidence of your innocence; but the more digging he did on you, the more he became convinced of your guilt. So his next step is to try to convince the Justice Department.

His comprehensive report to the government prosecutors will contain everything from your name and address to Exhibit Z. Special agents usually follow a format recommended by the IRS, but the exact order of items varies from district to district and agent to agent. In general each report contains the following, in roughly the order listed:

INTRODUCTION: This covers the type of case being presented and the prosecution years, recommended charges, investigating agents, method of proof used, method of evasion, returns filed, statutes of limitation that apply, venue, source of case, date of initial contact with taxpayer, constitutional advice given, power of attorney filed, revenue agent's recommendations, any civil actions taken including prior audits, and whether or not you have paid your additional taxes.

HISTORY OF TAXPAYER: Full name, aliases, date and place of birth, health, spouse, dependents, place of residence, education, military service, reputation in community, criminal actions (whether or not related to IRS crimes), business history, knowledge of tax matters, and any other pertinent data.

EVIDENCE OF INCOME: This section begins with the special agent's theory of case, which sums up the charges against you, evidence, dates, and how the IRS will prove their case. It goes on to list your books and records and how they were kept, who prepared and filed your returns and any instructions you gave, reconciliation of your records to your tax return, and an explanation of items appearing in the appendix, where your taxable income is calculated.

EVIDENCE OF INTENT: Remember, without intent, or wilfulness, there is no criminal case. The agent lists here all the statements made by you or other witnesses that indicate you knew you were evading taxes (or whatever they may be charging you with).

EXPLANATION AND DEFENSE OF TAXPAYER: Sometime during the investigation, perhaps more than once, the special agent asked you to explain apparent discrepancies or omissions. Anything you said in your own defense will probably be listed here, along with possible rebuttals the government could use.

CONCLUSIONS AND RECOMMENDATIONS: Some of the evidence against you may be quite circumstantial, while some will be very specific. Taken all together, it will represent enough proof to bring criminal charges. Here the special agent will cite the specific crime (s) he recommends you be charged with, and states his reasons.

LIST OF WITNESSES AND EXHIBITS: Everything relating to your case from handwritten receipts to your friendly neighborhood banker will be cited here, to be used as evidence or testimony at your trial.

If you thought the investigation took a long time, wait until you find out how long it takes the wheels of Justice to turn. It could be months or longer than a year before they act on the special agent's recommendation, either accepting or rejecting it. Meanwhile you are rapidly approaching the end of your rope, imagining all the terrible things they'll do to you if and when you're convicted. If only the trial could be over with, and your agony ended. Maybe there *is* a way out. . . .

You've always heard government officials were corruptible. Now might be a good time to offer this "poor" man a little "help." Yes, it may be possible to bribe some special agents out of your life, but if yours is one of those who goes by the book, beware! He's not going to refuse your subtle offer, but will arrange another meeting sometime in the near future, when you can get down to brass tacks (or silver ones, as the case may be). At that private meeting, thinking you're almost home free, you spell out your offer—and every word is tape-recorded by an officer from the Internal Security Division (the same folks you complain to if an IRS agent harasses you). When bribes are offered, agents are trained to stall the taxpayer until they can be wired for sound. The bribe offer is then used as evidence against you.

If your special agent seems like a "company man" who is above taking bribes, you may consider summoning your last ounce of courage and confessing. Donning your humblest of pitiful expressions and your meanest hair-shirt, you crawl contritely into the IRS office and seek that agent who sent you down the path to hell in the first place. Stifling the urge to lash out at him for causing you all these troubles, you meekly confess to your sins, beg to plead guilty, and offer your wrists for handcuffing until you throw yourself on the mercy of the court. It's one of your better performances, but the special agent is not impressed.

"And just what are you pleading guilty to?" he inquires, trying with all his might to conceal a grin threatening to explode into laughter.

"What . . . ?" you manage, your bubble of self-mortification bursting.

"How can you plead guilty," says the agent, "when you haven't been charged with anything yet?"

Oh-oh, you really did it to yourself this time. Well, you've gone this far, no turning back now. "Well, go ahead, charge me. Whatever it is, I did it, I confess. I'm guilty, and I'm sorry, and I'll never do it again. Here," you scream, emptying your pockets, "take it, take it all, and if I owe you any more, I'll pay that too. . . . Anything you want, just get off my back, pleeeeeeeeeeeaaase!!!"

And as they drag you, screaming and bawling, from the office, the special agent calmly adds your confession to his "intent" file, privately thanking you for making his job that much easier.

Of course, if you had volunteered your confession *before* you knew they would be investigating you, they might have looked more favorably upon your case, and chances are you'd have been spared the prosecution process. In fact, most IRS agents would have a hard time recalling anyone being prosecuted after making a voluntary disclosure. Timing is the crucial factor. Confess before the IRS contacts you, and your ordeal should be much easier and less costly. But if you wait until after the IRS contacts you, it will be taken as another item of intent that will strengthen the IRS case.

To enforce our many tax laws, we have the IRS. To enforce the criminal portions of the Tax Code, the IRS has its Criminal Investigation Division, consisting of about 2,500 highly trained special agents. Cases are usually referred to them by the Examination Division, but there are other conduits through which they can be channeled, too.

Once a special agent has been assigned to your case, he makes a thorough study of the IRS files on you and interviews the examiner who referred your case. This not only prepares him for his contacts with you, but gives him a chance to evaluate any weaknesses that might damage the case in court. During his first interview with you he'll try to pin you down on as many specifics as he can while you're still unprepared, ever alert to contradictions and items of intent. You yourself may not realize what the special agent is after, but a good attorney should be able to anticipate his moves. You should seriously consider contacting one before answering any questions (other than identifying yourself to the man with the badge) or submitting any records.

After interviewing the witnesses connected with your case, and examining all pertinent documents and other evidence, the special agent will write a comprehensive report which will include the criminal charges he recommends to the Justice Department. He could have dropped the case at any point along the line, if you had proved your innocence. If not, the case ambles its way slowly through the justice system; if they finally accept it, you will eventually be charged with a crime.

When it becomes known in your community that you are the subject of a criminal investigation, your prestige could sink so low you might consider bribing the agent or confessing, just to put an end to your agony. However, a confession at this point, after the investigation has already begun, would only serve as another item of intent; whereas, if you had come forward voluntarily—*before* they contacted you—they probably would have gone much easier on you. Of course, special agents will appreciate any outright admissions you care to make, which they will include in their report. That's what makes them so special.

AFTERWORD

As was stated at the outset, this book was written primarily to answer the most common questions taxpayers ask about the Internal Revenue Service. Some of the answers may have surprised you, others might have opened your eyes; some may be of little use to you, but here's hoping you picked up at least a few suggestions that will be of help.

You are bound to have other questions that this book left unanswered, or perhaps questions cropped up in your mind as you read. We don't pretend to have all the answers—no tax book can have. If you cannot find the information you seek in one of the publications referred to in the text, call the IRS or a good accountant or tax attorney.

The fact that you chose to read this book at all indicates your understanding of the most crucial element in any attempt to defend yourself against the IRS: knowledge. Now that you are no longer in the dark about such things as audits, penalties, appeal procedures, methods of proof, and criminal investigations, you deserve to feel much more confident about facing the IRS than do taxpayers who approach them from ignorance.

We sincerely hope your case never goes beyond an audit in which no adjustments are made. And if you're never called for an audit, so much the better! However, no matter how big a role the IRS plays in your life, at least you will be armed.

P.S. If this book has aided you in any way in preparing or verifying your tax return, you may count it as a deduction. Many happy returns!